Threshold God

Threshold God

Discovering Christ in the Margins of Life

CYRIL ASHTON

Foreword by Gerard W. Hughes

daybreak
London

First published in 1992 by
Daybreak
Darton, Longman and Todd Ltd
89 Lillie Road, London SW6 1UD

ISBN 0–232–51880–7

A catalogue record for this book is available
from the British Library

The scriptural quotations are taken from
The Holy Bible, New International Version
© 1973, 1978, 1984 by International Bible Society.
Thanks are also due to Burns & Oates for permission
to quote from E. Allison Peers' translation of
The Dark Night of the Soul by St John of the Cross.

Phototypeset by Intype, London
Printed and bound in Great Britain
at the University Press, Cambridge

For my mother
and for Steve and Rujon

Contents

Foreword

For a long time I have been reflecting on the fundamental dislocation which exists right at the heart of our contemporary spirituality. This dislocation enables us at a personal level to believe in a God who, on the one hand, is presented as all-loving, while on the other hand, is feared because of his imagined response to our weaknesses, failures and sins. A similar contradiction occurs at a global level when we blithely pray for world peace while at the same time endorse policies which create the means for massive human destruction. Our spirituality is split because we keep God at a safe distance from our everyday affairs. This may appear to foster reverence, but is, in fact, a refusal to let God be the God who makes himself known in Jesus.

We keep God at a distance, not only because we fear his reaction to the shadow side of our personalities, but also because his presence disturbs our complacency. To pray for the hungry to be fed, the homeless sheltered, and the sick and aged cared for, without doing what we can to make this happen, is evidence of a split spirituality. Allowing Christ access to the margins of our lives, where these contradictions and ambiguities occur, would undoubtedly reintegrate our attitudes, values, priorities and ways of behaving. We would be well on the way to a healing of our spirituality which would, in turn, lead to an increase of appropriate self-love, as well as channelling more genuine, practical love for others.

I have also thought about this split in relation to emotional and psychological health. When discussing the matter with a group of Christian psychotherapists I discovered that, even when they were working with Christian clients, they did not encourage them to bring their psychological problems into prayer, or to reflect on them in the light of it. The reason they gave was that if they were to encourage their clients to pray, they would do so all too readily, and find in prayer an escape route from having to confront the reality of their own problems. This was a sad confirmation of my suspicion that we are working with a split spirituality: we dare not let God, the ultimate loving reality, be God to our most intimate and secret problems concealed in the hidden margins of our lives.

In *Threshold God*, Cyril Ashton presents a God who is, in St Augustine's words, closer to us than we are to ourselves, and who, in St Paul's words, 'became sin for us'. He is a God who is most powerful in our weakness and darkness, provided we acknowledge it and so encounter his mercy, compassion and tenderness there. This is a book which helps to heal the split in our spirituality.

GERARD W. HUGHES

Acknowledgements

I am grateful to a number of people for the help they have given me as I have worked on this book. I especially want to thank my wife Muriel, my daughter Elizabeth, Hilary Hopwood, Sue Hunt, Jill Bundy, Anita Compton, Sue Kiernan and Val Snelling for reading the text and making constructive comments. Anne Adams has worked patiently typing the manuscript for publication. I am very grateful to her. My friend, David Carroll, has given a lot of time and skill to help me clarify the material for the book – I owe him special thanks. Thanks are also due to my editor at DLT, Morag Reeve; she has been encouraging and supportive throughout. Above all, she has been gracious when deadlines have not been met. Also, my love and thanks to Jonathan, Elizabeth, Simon and Timothy, whose good-humoured support and enthusiastic attitude to life have helped me to see my own thresholds more clearly.

Introduction

We all have fears, temptations, unfulfilled desires, strong off-centre instincts which strain against established boundaries of acceptability. In constantly repeated acts of self-delusion we push our unholy thoughts and unworthy motives away from the centre towards the shadowy margins of our being. The fringes of our minds are cluttered with the part-submerged wrecks of shameful past deeds. Our dreams and guilty memories give us occasional fearful glimpses into this murky borderland, but we dare not linger, afraid to face the pain and confusion it represents. A considerable proportion of our thought life and hidden motivation stems from the experiences and memories which we have concealed in these shrouded darkened margins. We would not like other people to know what is buried there, and, instinctively, we feel that the existence of this no-man's land makes us unacceptable to God.

There is, however, a very important truth to acknowledge. On earth Jesus spent much of his time in the margins of human society. He refused to allow himself to be cloistered in the safe centre of a religious community, but spent his time at the fringes, bringing love and forgiveness to the outcast and the shamed. The sinner who finds himself outside the church, and perhaps even marginalized by human society, is the specific object of his love. Christ was to be found as often with prostitutes as with Pharisees.

The central act of the Christian faith took place outside a city wall. This is most significant. Calvary is the place where human sin and guilt are met with love and forgiveness. It is the event which transforms the margins into a threshold. The cross symbolizes for all time that God meets us in the place of shame and failure, turning defeat into life and growth.

This book is about the God of the Threshold, the One who gives us courage to face the darkened outer edges of our human experience. Gently he enables us to accept that failure, fear and shame, far from being factors that distance us from God, are in themselves passageways of transformation. The dark, outer edges of life are no longer to be seen as a feared burial ground of unwelcome thoughts and desires, but as a threshold to new life and growth. From the rubbish heap outside the city wall emerges the new life of Easter.

This principle of turning shame and defeat into growth is fundamental to our understanding of the God of the Bible. We are given a new philosophy of life, a new way of understanding our relationship with God and with each other, and a new hope that those things which have previously held us back can become the starting-point for fresh progress. God turns things inside out. With him the shadowy margins of life become the threshold through which we move into greater wholeness.

A word of explanation about the use of the threshold metaphor in the following chapters. A threshold stands between the inside and the outside, separating one world or reality from another. Because of this, crossing a threshold is a movement of uncertainty, a stepping out from the known to the unknown. We have to cross thresholds, to take risks, in order that we might grow. Some threshold experiences are formalized as rites of passage; baptism, confirmation, and marriage would be examples of this. But of equal, perhaps even greater, significance are our own personal thresholds which invite us into deeper wholeness and knowledge of God. Such thresholds present themselves as we face the unacceptable, shadowy margins of our human experience, and beckon us forwards, as the People of the Way, on a pilgrimage of hope.

I shall be seeking to apply these insights in a practical way, exploring important biblical truths to do with self-knowledge, our relationship with God and our relationship with others. I hope also in the process to lay to rest some of the myths, accumulated around a false view of God, which have led to unreal expectations of ordinary human nature. Such myths have kept alive guilt and fear, and have prevented us from enjoying the greatest gift of all; the freedom of a joyful, surprising, liberating relationship with God.

1

The Search for God

An attractive young middle-aged woman asked to see me. She told me of the breakdown of her marriage, of the confusion, pain and lostness she experienced. She told me also of her relentless search for love, for acceptance and understanding. As she talked her face betrayed a restless sadness that I have seen many times in others. It is the sadness of an unfulfilled life, of dashed expectations, of dreams trampled in the dust. The human heart searches for love with astonishing tenacity. To be loved wholly and completely for what we are in ourselves, to have someone with whom to share our dreams, that is the goal towards which we strive.

Having failed in this quest some invest their longings in achievements, possessions or charitable works, seeing in these things another possible route towards the same goal. At the end of the day, unsatisfied, our inner loneliness is recognized and feared, our faces reflecting the still unmatched yearning within. Karl Rahner speaks of 'the torment of the insufficiency of everything attainable'.

We are in one state or condition and think that fulfilment can be found by entering a different state or condition. The unmarried person, therefore, seeks to be married, transferring onto his partner an impossible burden. The married, having expected marriage to end loneliness, find even greater isolation and seek solutions in a series of new relationships.

St Augustine once prayed, 'You have made us for yourself, Lord, and our hearts are restless until they rest in you.' The answer to some of life's most difficult questions is often pro-

foundly simple. Our hunger for love can only partially be met
by people, and must be met supremely by God. Jesus said, 'I
am the bread of life. He who comes to me will never go hungry,
and he who believes in me will never be thirsty' (John 6:35).

Human nature thrives on complications. We cannot believe
that the solution to our deepest personal needs can be found
in meeting with God. We cannot accept, or do so only with
difficulty, that this inner restlessness, this unfulfilled yearning
which has driven and tormented us for so long may be God's
way of drawing us to himself. It is a gift not a curse.

In the mythology of love the hero expects to run the gauntlet
of near-impossible tasks in order to win love. From childhood
onwards, we seek to prove love by erecting barriers to determine its genuineness. From whichever direction we come,
whether to give or receive love, we expect, and often create,
obstacles. A person who has sought to attract love from another
and has spent much of his conscious and subconscious energy
in this pursuit, finds it hard to believe that love is given by God
for no other reason than that he is. Because I am, the love of
God is focused upon me. No persuasion is necessary.

God's love is not conditional, there are no obstacles except
those of our own making. If only we could truly grasp this fact
there would be a transformation of restlessness into peace,
sadness into joy, and of searching into being found. However,
in our search for God, we meet with uncertain signposting.

A Too-human View of God's Love

We dare not believe we can receive unconditional love from
God because we perceive him as being personal in the same
way that we are personal. At an intellectual level, of course,
most Christians would accept that God is all-loving, but at the
level of experience we fear that his personality may have the
same flaws as our own. We expect conditional love, i.e. he will
love us if we are good, and, as a rule, we expect disapproval.

This would be very simple to test. Next time you are conscious of offending God, reflect on your reactions to the event. Many would brace themselves for a rebuke and expect that in some way God will either withdraw his favour or be cold. Even after having assented to the truth of the unchangeable nature of God and his unending forgiveness, we would nevertheless expect to be sent out of his presence. 'Go to your bedroom and do without your tea' is the human echo of this experience.

Obviously we can get glimpses of God's personality through insights given to us by our own. But that does not exhaust his meaning. God is not small or finite, he is not ungrateful or greedy, selfish or resentful. He is not capricious or moody, truculent or sulky. He does not spend time thinking of ways to pay us back when we sin against him. We need to recognize what is happening. When we speak of God as a person we subconsciously project on to him our negative human characteristics. So we expect him to respond to us as anyone else might.

'Your thoughts of God are too human,' Luther told Erasmus. This is precisely the issue. We think of God as having all the limitations of being human. In this context we dare not expose our weaknesses to God. We hide the more shameful and unworthy elements of our lives from him as though he were no more capable of accepting them than the people closest to us. The dark boundaries of our lives, the outer edges constitute a no-man's land from which even God is excluded.

There is in many of us an implicit belief that God's love is limited. Our disappointments and fears experienced in human love are transferred to God. We do not really expect him to do any better. Recognizing this, we are faced with even more uncertain signposting in our search for God.

Even in the richest of human loves we find an incompleteness. It might be helpful to look at some of the limitations in human love which have shaped our understanding, or misunderstanding, of God's love.

The Fragility of Human Love

Part of the limitation of human love is its *fragility*. When my children were very young I learned an important lesson. We lived in a house which had a large garden containing some lovely fruit trees. In season, local youngsters visited our garden to engage in the age-old pursuit of helping themselves to apples. I did not mind that, people with fruit trees are fair game. What I did object to was the fact that the raiders repeatedly and deliberately damaged both the fence and the trees. One day I devised a plan to teach them a lesson. Suspecting they might come on a particular night I ran the garden hose-pipe from a tap in the house and concealed it down a line of trees to the likely scene of the next crime. The idea was to watch and wait for the intruders to get into the garden and climb the trees, then to hose them down. With great excitement my children and I set the trap.

That night, at family prayers, our eldest son, who was about five years old, prayed this prayer. 'Dear Lord, please make those boys come tonight, so that daddy can get them with the hose-pipe.' It was funny and we laughed about it. Afterwards, however, I felt uncomfortable. The lesson I was teaching them was an unpleasant one. That my neighbourly goodwill soon gave way to vengeance when someone took liberties with me. The implicit lesson taught at family prayers was that God seemed to endorse my vindictiveness. Happily the intruders did not come.

I have subsequently realized that for a very long time I believed that God did act vengefully. When I offended him I waited for him to get back at me as though he operated crudely at the human level of tit for tat. No wonder we feel uneasy when God looks into the margins of our lives, noting the evil, the inconsistencies and the general level of nastiness that exists. We wait fearfully for his judgement to fall.

The Insecurity of Human Love

Human love frequently sets narrow limits, seeking to bring under control, or manipulate, the person loved. In essence this is an attempt to make sure we do not lose. Such love will not take risks because it cannot survive unless it is the centre of attention. We may feel disquiet when the person, who is the object of our love, expresses independence as though that were a threat to our position in their affections. Typically therefore, we devise means of making sure the other person always notices us, always defers to us, and always puts us first. This is a form of possession, based on insecurity, which robs the person loved of any freedom. In a real sense that person ceases to be an 'other', but rather has become a devalued, and later despised, extension of oneself.

We can become expert at controlling others by the use of actions which appear to be selfless. A mother will warn her child about the risks of contact with particular friends. On the surface concern is being expressed about the dangers such friendships may contain, underneath, a statement is being made about the fear of losing power. A similar factor is often at work when a person insists on fulfilling tasks which appear to offer a service to others, but in reality make them dependent. C. S. Lewis wrote of a woman who lived for others, wryly observing that you could tell who the 'others' were by their hunted look.

Secretly, we know the lengths to which we will go in order to control and manipulate other people. Much conversation contains hidden meanings, and sometimes hidden threats, directed against courses of action that may lead others to independence. We do not want other people to manage without us, and we tie them to us by guilt on the pretext that we cannot manage without them. Many seem bound to God by guilt rather than love. Perhaps, in talking about the human qualities of God, we have transferred to him this controlling, manipulative quality. We fear that we will lose our freedom, our independence, our individuality and will be tied to him in a way that restricts our growth and inhibits our personalities. We inwardly decide that God will not understand our need for independence and freedom, he will not understand our dreams and our longings.

Unadventurous Human Love

We offer, as far as we are able, our greatest love to someone and it goes unmatched. We long for a reciprocal richness, frequently to be disappointed. No one else can think our great thoughts, dream our great dreams, or understand us as we want to be understood. Experience of life has taught us this, and we fear that God will not understand either, or even worse, will consider our human aspirations too trivial to bother with.

One of Ireland's greatest poets, W. B. Yeats, wrote,

> But I being poor, have only my dreams.
> I have spread my dreams under your feet;
> tread softly, because you tread on my dreams.

We dare not think that our dreams might find an approving echo in the heart of God.

We feel he will want to control us, clip our wings, rebuke us for our silliness. The religious principles of duty and thrift are deeply rooted in us. Commendable as they are they do not express the totality of life. God, we are led to believe, is interested only in the mundane and ordinary, all else is frivolous and unworthy. Thus, our creative vital joy is diminished and our dreams and visions choked at birth. Because we do not truly know God we fear he will trample on our dreams. Utilitarian principles have so infiltrated the Christian tradition that we cannot imagine God being remotely interested in our dreams.

Pressure to conform to religious and social norms of behaviour has inhibited much legitimate expression of personality. We soon learn that anything out of the ordinary is regarded with suspicion, and pressure to conform is quickly brought to bear. So people with rich and varied personalities, who may have different ways of doing and saying things, feel themselves to be suppressed and constrained by other people's disapproval.

Discipline, responsibility, and a commitment to serve one another in practical ways are indispensable marks of Christian life and must not be devalued. Obedience to God's Word and sensitivity to others are similarly binding upon us, shaping us to fit into the Christian community. But also, we need to set each other free to be the people God created us to be. We must not allow the church to destroy or inhibit God's gift to each person, by insisting on some pallid universal standard of mediocrity. The unique and lovely qualities in each person must be allowed expression. We need to give permission to each other to dream dreams. Instead, we trample on each other's dreams and expect God to do the same.

An incident occurs in John's Gospel which illustrates this point. Mary, out of sheer love for Jesus, makes an extravagant gesture anointing his feet with very expensive perfume and then wiping his feet with her hair. Here is a human being following a profound instinct to offer love and worship in a uniquely personal, different, even sensual way. One of the disciples reduces this lovely moment, and dismisses it, by making a purely utilitarian comparison. 'Why wasn't this perfume sold and the money given to the poor?' Whatever the motive, and we know in this instance it was personal greed, the response was to devalue an act which obviously sprang from Mary's heart. It encourages me enormously to note that Jesus received Mary's offering with joy and pleasure. He was willing to let her be herself and accepted her generous offering of love.

In our ordinary human relationships there is pressure to strangle at birth our generous, loving instincts. A husband may want to buy his wife an extravagant gift, but in the end is dissuaded by lack of nerve or by financial constraint. We may want to say something encouraging to someone else, or may want to give them flowers, but decide against it because it appears to cross the threshold of convention. Our loving is limited, restricted and controlled because we fear it will be misunderstood or rejected. Subconsciously we feel that God's love is similarly unadventurous, restricted and controlled.

The Vulnerability of Human Love

A further constraint on human love is that of vulnerability. So often hurt, we have built barriers for protection. We make ourselves invulnerable, and recognize that many we meet day to day have followed a similar process. Instead of openness and warmth in our relationships, there is suspicion and fear. Frequently, one gets the feeling that one is not meeting the person, but a defended citadel. Pressure of time, tiredness, and being taken for granted are all factors which contribute to the layers of protection we build around ourselves. What we do not always understand is that the walls of protection which make us safe from hurt, also prevent us from receiving love. Hurting and loving are two sides of the same coin. C. S. Lewis once said that the only place we are safe from the dangers of love is Hell.

One cannot know love without making oneself vulnerable to being hurt. Often hurt itself is a painful reminder of the love we fear does not exist. A child will sometimes go to extreme lengths to provoke anger, and is curiously reassured because somewhere deep down he perceives that the angry reaction is evidence of his parents' care. This can have an extraordinary and unexpected healing effect. Frequently we interpret anger as rejection when it is likely to be the opposite. When God is angry, and sometimes we know this is so, he is angry at our sin. It is not because he rejects us, but precisely because he loves us.

Authentic love carries with it great power. The power to disturb or to make peaceful, to cause pain or joy. It is the power to affect another at the deepest possible level. In W. H. Vanstone's words it is the 'power of meaning'. The lover, in order truly to love, must remain vulnerable. God longs to meet our needs, not defend himself against them.

The Self-centredness of Human Love

Underlying many of our difficulties in human relationships is the instinct for self-preservation. Positive in many ways it can, and often does, go beyond its basic purpose, affecting relationships in a negative way. Every good quality can be carried to extremes so that it becomes destructive. An entirely proper instinct for self-preservation can be perverted into self-centredness. The lover when she offers authentic love gives a person power over herself. The self-interested person does not confer that power because she fears she will be disadvantaged. Dietrich Bonhoeffer wrote, 'Satan's desire is to turn me in on myself to the extent that I become a destructive force in the community. The thrust from Jesus is the opposite – to enhance my freedom so that I can become a creative force of love. It is the spirit of self-centredness and selfishness versus the spirit of openness and self-sacrifice for the good of others.'

Self-centredness destroys love because it always needs praise. The self-interested person is nurtured on the applause of others and constantly manipulates situations to become the focus of attention. Such a person is not really interested in the good qualities of others, except that noting them, they make him jealous. He cannot bear to hear another person praised. Clamouring for recognition, this person becomes sullen and depressed when none is forthcoming. Another's downfall or pain almost always causes a secret feeling of pleasure.

Knowing this, the biblical command to praise God can be confusing and is often met with suspicion. Does God need to be praised? Knowing that our longing for praise is sometimes a result of personal insecurity, do we conclude that God is similarly insecure? Secretly we all despise people who are seeking continual statements of their importance. We find it distasteful that some seem to go out of their way to invite adulation. Moreover, we despise the unexpressed jealousy that wells up within us when another is applauded instead of ourselves. Is God like this, with an insatiable and thoroughly repugnant need to be constantly praised?

C. S. Lewis confessed that this was a great stumbling block to him coming to faith. Not only that he should be told by other Christians that he should praise God, but also that God himself demanded it. In his view it was hideously like God saying, 'What I want most is to be told that I am good and great.' Understanding came to him when he realized that it is not merely as a compliment that lovers keep on telling one another how beautiful they are; delight is incomplete until it is expressed. In commanding us to praise him, God is inviting us to enjoy him, to delight ourselves in him. This is pure gift.

It is a great loss to us if we fail to seek God because we mistrust his motives in demanding our praise. God is personal, but he is personal in a way that transcends our ordinary human understanding of personality. Our fear that he will be unable to accept us because of our threshold emotions, our dark and off-centre desires, are totally groundless. In the next chapter I will try to explore this theme further by considering some aspects of the character of God as revealed in the Bible, especially through the person of Christ.

2

A Ridiculous Love

We fear condemnation from God because we transfer onto him the limitations we find in human love. God is the author and giver of love, so his love must be the same as ours. Without recognizing what we are doing we conclude that his love also is precarious, restricted and variable. Instinctively we set out to win God's love as we would human love and establish an elaborate system of tasks and tests in order to merit God's favour. The church, in a whole variety of different ways, has co-operated in this process. In order to win human love we court the attention and affection of the beloved, promising gifts and undertaking exploits, even experiencing pain, to demonstrate our worthiness. The would-be lover will invite, even demand, that tasks be prescribed in order to test the quality and superiority of the love offered. We slip into the same attitude in our relationship with God. We feel his love has to be won, that he must be persuaded that we are worthy of his attention.

Small wonder that we concentrate on presenting our best side to him, concealing, or attempting to conceal, our unacceptable shadow as though it were a blemish that would offend God and cause him to withdraw. I once heard an elderly man protest that he would not go forward to receive Holy Communion because he felt so unworthy. First, he believed, he must tidy up his life and make himself acceptable to God. I told him he was never more worthy, and never more loved by God than at that moment. Our failures are probably the only genuine things we can offer God and he is willing to receive us immediately we trust him with them. This is how Bishop John Taylor expressed it:

> The whole doctrine of justification by faith hinges, for me, upon my painfully reluctant realisation that my Father is not going to be any more pleased with me when I am good than he is now when I am bad. He accepts me and delights in me as I am. It is ridiculous of him, but that is how it is between us.[1]

To believe in a God who is limited by our understanding of human love is to believe in a false God. When we see Jesus in the New Testament we see him, not protected from the people who considered themselves failures, but earnestly seeking them out. Characteristically, he would be mixing with prostitutes, thieves, frauds and adulterers. He offered unconditional and unlimited love to the loveless. Confounding human wisdom, religious and social acceptability, he repeatedly crossed the threshold into the shadowlands of human life, taking the transforming love of God to those who did not deserve it and who had no way of earning it.

I find this profoundly encouraging. If this is the nature of God's love I dare to ask him into the twilight areas of my own mind and heart, exposing to him the hiddenness in the shadowlands of my personality. God is personal, but his personality cannot be defined and his meaning exhausted by reference to the human personality. God is love, but his love is not limited according to our experience of human love.

The Greatness of God

God is present with us, but he is also 'other'. The Bible speaks frequently of the majesty, the greatness of God. Some years ago a book was published with the title, *Your God Is Too Small*. This describes the belief of many Christians. In focusing on the personal, we have made God personal like us, small-minded, petty, needing to be handled carefully lest he is offended. 'We are modern men', wrote Jim Packer, 'and modern men, though they cherish great thoughts of man, have as a rule small thoughts of God.' God has made himself access-ible to us, the incarnation is the supreme proof of this fact – but he is God. The prophet Isaiah expressed it in this way: ' "For my thoughts are not your thoughts, neither are your ways my ways," declares the Lord. "As the heavens are higher than the earth so are my ways higher than your ways, and my thoughts than your thoughts" ' (Isaiah 55:8,9).

Whatever else this may mean, it certainly means that God does not react to us in merely human ways. Offended by some-one, we might be tempted to put them down. God would not stoop to that. His thoughts and his ways are higher than ours. Jesus exemplified this when he refused to retaliate or justify himself when condemned and accused. He taught it, in a most astonishing way, when he commanded us to love our enemies. A typical human reaction would be to love our friends and hate our enemies. To do that, however, is to do no more than follow natural laws. Jesus said, 'Love your enemies and pray for those who persecute you' (Matthew 5:44). It is a sign of God's greatness that he continues to love whatever the response. If he commands me to love my enemies, he must be willing to go on loving me even though parts of my life are at enmity with him.

God's greatness, his otherness, assures his continuous love. Because we are fickle, variable and touchy we must not assume that God is also. He is not to be compared with humankind. 'Human love needs human meriting', wrote Francis Thompson in his poem 'The Hound of Heaven', but God's love requires no such human meriting. God is God. ' "To whom will you compare me? Or who is my equal?" says the Holy One' (Isaiah 40:25). This question rebukes our small thoughts about God. He is not like a human being to grow tired and disillusioned. He cannot forget or abandon us, or lose interest in us. Our

God is too small when we fail to acknowledge the reality of his limitless love and power. The prophet Isaiah gives a true perspective.

> Do you not know?
>   Have you not heard?
> The Lord is the everlasting God,
>   the Creator of the ends of the earth.
> He will not grow tired or weary,
>   and his understanding no-one can fathom.
> He gives strength to the weary
>   and increases the power of the weak.
> Even youths grow tired and weary,
>   and young men stumble and fall;
> but those who hope in the Lord
>   will renew their strength.
> They will soar on wings like eagles;
>   they will run and not grow weary,
> they will walk and not be faint.
>
> (Isaiah 40:28–31)

The Faithfulness of God

We can further explore the theme of the 'otherness' of God as a person, by talking of the faithfulness of God. He does not go back on his promises concerning us. Again, Isaiah speaks clearly: ' "Though the mountains be shaken and the hills be removed, yet my unfailing love for you will not be shaken nor my covenant of peace be removed," says the Lord, who has compassion on you' (Isaiah 54:10).

The theme of the faithfulness of God recurs time and time again in the Bible. We cannot wear out his patience. We frequently talk about our commitment to God. We need, however, to recognize the primary truth of his commitment to us.

Nothing can separate us from his love. This truth is forcibly expressed by St Paul.

> For I am convinced that neither death nor life, neither angels nor demons, neither the present nor the future, nor any powers, neither height nor depth, nor anything else in all creation, will be able to separate us from the love of God that is in Christ Jesus our Lord. (Romans 8:38–9)

The thought that we must be perfect in order to attract God's love is a thought drawn from our human understanding of love. God is faithful to us as his children. Whether we are good or bad children, nothing alters the fact that we are his children and remain the objects of his love. In the parable of the Prodigal Son the faithfulness of God is seen in the joy of the father at the return of the son. His love had never wavered.

I find this comforting in Christian ministry. Knowing the responsibilities I have, and knowing the sin of my own heart, I would despair if I could not rely on God's faithfulness. I need to know he will continue loving me and using me even though I fail. Accepting this fact, I am still curiously reluctant to live as though it were true. When I let God down I feel that he will not want to continue to use me.

In Christian marriage the couple commit themselves to each other 'for better or worse'. Marriage is expected to endure even if it should turn out to be worse rather than better. We would not expect God to offer a lesser form of love than that. He is faithful to us for better or worse. This explains a phenomenon that often puzzles Christians. Why is it that a person can still be used significantly by God even though his or her personal life is in a mess? The answer is to do with the faithfulness of God.

Despite the fact that we say we believe in the grace of God, many still live as though they have to earn their righteousness. Gifts and ministries are given in response to faith and because of the grace of God. They are not rewards for good behaviour.

The gifts and call of God are irrevocable simply because he is faithful. We may turn out to be worse, rather than better, but this will not shake his covenanted love. If it were left to us we would hand out God's gifts on a reward basis. God does not do that. Similarly, if someone, in our view, was not earning the right to use those gifts, we would withdraw them. God does not do that either. Having committed himself to us he does not withdraw, he remains faithful. In this way also he is 'other'.

Francis Thompson was derelict, his life was packed with pain and shame. He was a man running away from God. He wrote an extraordinarily powerful poem, 'The Hound of Heaven', in which the theme of God's faithfulness, mercy, and generous love is vividly captured.

> I fled Him down the nights and down the days;
>   I fled Him down the arches of the years;
> I fled Him down the labyrinthine ways
>   Of my own mind; and in the midst of tears
> I hid from Him, and under running laughter.
>   Up vistaed hopes I sped;
>   And shot, precipitated,
>   Adown Titanic glooms of chasmed fears,
> From those strong Feet that followed, followed after.[2]

In these verses all the fears of one who cannot bear God to see into the shadows of his life are expressed passionately. Unable to open up our inner life to him we run from him, and in the running heap upon ourselves more fears and torments, as with mindless haste we seek to elude him. There is security, even in the dark things in our lives. They are at least familiar, and to have them exposed to the light and then removed, flings us into hopeless panic. Even though we acknowledge God's purposes of love, still we fear him.

> For though I knew His Love who followed,
>   Yet was I sore adread
> Lest, having Him, I must have naught beside.

Having reduced God to our level we dread his response to our failures. Inwardly we brace ourselves for judgement and for the loss of his love.

> 'Whom wilt thou find to love ignoble thee
>   Save Me, save only Me?
> All which I took from thee I did but take,
>   Not for thy harms,
> But just that thou might'st seek it in My arms.
>   All which thy child's mistake
> Fancies as lost, I have stored for thee at home;
>   Rise, clasp My hand, and come!'

The history of God's dealings with his people reveals his total faithfulness. He is faithful in his undiminished desire to give. God pursues us, not to deny us, but to fulfil us. The incarnation of Christ bears radical witness to God's determination to continue his faithfulness towards us. In a real sense it can be interpreted as God pursuing us in order to bestow his gift of life. Christian tradition has preserved an idea of God as mean and vengeful, who, if he bothered with us at all, would do so only to rebuke and to punish. The reverse is the case. He pursues us in order to complete our joy, to bless us with his forgiveness and his love. God constantly initiates contact with us in order to fulfil his promises. In our search for God we make a surprising discovery. He is already searching for us.

The Generosity of God

It is a remarkable truth that God pursues us, not to take away but to give. His love is utterly and overwhelmingly generous. He is not reluctant to part with his favours, nor does he require heroic efforts on our part to please him. My view is that we do not ask enough. I know as a father myself it is a great joy to be able to give things to my children. It gives me pleasure to plan surprises, to give unexpectedly and generously. Surely God's love cannot be less than that of an earthly father? Simone Weil writes, 'We have an unlimited right to ask God for everything that is good. In such demands there is no need for humility or moderation.'[3]

If we stopped to think about it, we would soon realize that the New Testament paints a picture of a Father who is overwhelmingly, even ridiculously, generous. In the parable of the Prodigal Son we see the essence of this love displayed. Given the circumstances of a son running away from home, wasting huge amounts of his father's hard-earned money, any father would have been justified simply to welcome his son home after having disgraced the family in this way. But it was not like that. While the son was wasting himself, his father's resources and reputation, his father was watching and waiting for his return. Seeing his son returning, he ran to him, making his love abundantly clear. In welcoming the son back across the threshold, the father moved his own boundaries. In the East a great person would always walk, never run. The father ran, his joy causing him to lay aside social convention, in order to show pleasure at his son's return. The father shifted his own boundaries further by giving an unconditional welcome and by reinstating his son in the heart of the family. Expecting to be received grudgingly, the son was prepared to come back on any terms, even as a servant. There was no rebuke, no reluctance, no probationary period, simply a joyful reunion, marked by love and overwhelming generosity. Having given his son what he had previously asked for, he now gave him what he dare not ask for, and had no right to expect.

This is the point at which we recognize divine love in action. God is willing to give far more than we ever dare ask or think. The father in this parable was not only determined to show generosity, but also refused to allow anyone to diminish his generosity. Even the grumbling complaint of his older son was met with similar generosity, 'All that I have is yours.'

Clearly God's desire is that we should count on his generosity, and that generosity should be the mark of our dealings with each other. It isn't enough to refuse to speak against another person, one must be prepared to speak generously of them. It isn't enough for a couple merely to be faithful, they must give themselves generously to each other. Such generosity of spirit reflects the generous heart of God.

This story is told of St Francis of Assisi. One rainy morning he entered a village and approached the piazza where the church was located. A crowd followed him chanting, 'Santo, santo, holy one'. The villagers knew that the local priest had not been living a life of moral rectitude. As Francis reached the piazza the priest happened to come out of the church. The crowd watched in tense silence. What would Francis do? Denounce the priest for the scandal he had caused? Sermonize the villagers on the nature of human frailty and the need for compassion? Simply ignore the priest and continue on his way? Francis stepped forward, knelt in the mud, took the priest's hand and kissed it. That is all, a beautifully generous gesture that showed respect and love.

To those who have fallen, Jesus acts in redeeming, liberating, generous compassion. Inviting repentance, he did so in a way which enabled his joy to enter the darkness of a person's life, thus giving hope.

The Divine Lover

It has been said that prayer is 'heart speaking to heart' as though we enter into communion with our Divine Lover. God beckons us joyfully in order to delight us with his love. We have divinized utilitarian thoughts of God, and so fail dismally to recognize him for who he is: the Divine Lover.

One of the most powerful images given in the Bible is of the church as the Bride of Christ. Some texts emphasize the fact that the individual Christian is the bride, and others that the church as a whole is the bride. There is no contradiction, the

symbolism is the same for both and paints a striking picture.
It deliberately evokes both the language and the relationship,
the lover and the beloved. With that in mind St Paul wrote to
the Corinthian Christians, 'I am jealous for you with a godly
jealousy. I promised you to one husband, to Christ, so that I
might present you as a pure virgin to him' (2 Corinthians 11:2).

The bridegroom-bride relationship is repeatedly used in the
Bible to illustrate the type of relationship we are to have with
God. The Song of Songs beautifully develops this theme. It
begins, 'Let him kiss me with the kisses of his mouth – for your
love is more delightful than wine' (Song 1:2). In this way
the Bible takes a common, but exceptionally powerful human
experience and presents it as a model to mark the way for us
to enter more completely into a relationship with God.

This cannot be dismissed as romanticism for two reasons.
First, considerable emphasis is placed on it in the Bible.
Second, being in love is the most compelling of all human
experiences. There is nothing greater, more exciting, more
consuming, more painful, or more fulfilling than being in love.
Once its imagery has been evoked as a means of explaining
God's love for us, it cannot be subordinated to any other image.
The person in love sees everything and everyone through the
filter of this experience. It is a transcendent experience.
Dietrich Bonhoeffer described it as an encounter which makes
people lose contact with the world around them. The lovers
begin by seeing only themselves in the world. In describing
this, there is unexpected agreement between popular love songs
and the greatest romantic poetry ever written. Both use
absolute terms to describe an experience which is total, and
which becomes a framework in which all other experiences are
placed and subordinated. Love is the light by which the lovers
perceive and assess everything else. It is a consuming, passion-
ate insatiable longing.

In this relationship all reserve vanishes; dark secrets, which
have been carefully hidden from everyone else, will be shared
without shame or fear of reproach. There is no detail so insig-

nificant that is unworthy of comment. To see a flower, grass-hopper, or sunset, is sufficient to want to share it with the beloved.

This is the relationship God beckons us into with him, the Lover and the Beloved, the Bridegroom and the Bride. Knowing this, I dare to let him into the margins of my life, to push away the sombre drapes that guard my most shameful secrets, and to allow the piercing sweetness of his love to reach me as a total human being.

One of the most evocative and imaginative pieces of religious poetry ever written came from St John of the Cross. In it the relationship between God and the believer as Lover and Beloved is expressed in a magnificent and beautiful way. St John of the Cross was a human being who had fallen in love with God.

On a dark night,
Kindled in love with yearnings – oh happy chance! –
I went forth without being observed,
My house being now at rest.

In darkness and secure,
By the secret ladder, disguised – oh, happy chance! –
In darkness and in concealment,
My house being now at rest.

In the happy night,
In secret, when none saw me,
Nor I beheld aught,
Without light or guide, save that which burned in my heart.

This light guided me
More surely than the light of noonday.
To the place where he (well I knew who!) was awaiting me
  –
A place where none appeared.

Oh, night that guided me,

Oh, night more lovely than the dawn,
Oh, night that joined Beloved with Lover, Lover
    transformed in the Beloved!

Upon my flowery breast, kept wholly for himself alone,
There he stayed sleeping, and I caressed him,
And the fanning of the cedars made a breeze.

The breeze blew from the turret as I parted his locks;
With his gentle hand he wounded my neck.
And caused all my senses to be suspended.

I remained, lost in oblivion;
My face I reclined on the Beloved.
All ceased and I abandoned myself, leaving my cares
    forgotten among the lilies.[4]

3

Downwardly Mobile

An Old Problem

Many of us have a double problem. Not only have we accepted an inadequate view of God, but also, we secretly hold an exalted view of ourselves – especially in relationship with others. We are walking paradoxes of inadequacy and superiority. These two powerful emotional states compete for dominance in personalities which, on the one hand, think themselves unworthy of God's love, while, on the other, frequently think themselves superior to other human beings. The insistence of our rights over those of another is a frequent clue to the reality of these feelings. Examine your reaction next time someone takes advantage of you, perhaps by barging in front of you in a queue, or infringing your personal comfort in some way.

All of us know the anger and indignation that rise up when someone takes advantage of us. Life is made up of many such incidents which fester and rankle, significantly spoiling the quality of daily life.

Generally, although it is hard to admit, we envy strength, we look up to people who have status and position, and we despise weakness. Much of our energy is spent in jockeying for position in society and making sure things go our way in personal relationships. Our instincts for self-assertion are keenly developed, though sometimes hidden or disguised in religious jargon. Some people have developed their skills to such an extent that they can get their own way even by pretending to be weak.

There may well be good reason for this state of affairs. Most people have sustained hurts through their lifetime because they have been trampled on, despised or marginalized in some way. There is a curious merry-go-round effect in human relationships. We feel put-down by others and consequently develop attitudes that harden us to those around us, perpetuating an instinct that operates to keep us on top, thus making it difficult for us to give way.

What we don't often realize is that such a way of life also hardens us against an experience of God. If we find it hard to give in to each other we will find it equally hard to give in to God.

Our instincts for self-preservation are so finely tuned that they will pick up and react to the merest flicker of a threat to our self-esteem. We need to be rid of the terrible burden of always feeling that we must get our own way. Innumerable relationship problems occur and are perpetuated because we do not have the grace to give in to another person for fear of losing face. We feel that unless we stay on top we will be devalued and trodden down into nothingness.

This fear of being a nobody is at the heart of many human conflicts and raises up in all of us an ugly and destructive obsession with our rights; our way; our voice to be heard.

A New Understanding

There is, of course, a proper self-love, an appropriate and necessary form of assertiveness, but when fear of being put down causes us to over-react and seek to dominate others, relationships can never have a proper footing and will limp along from one disaster to another.

God created us as part of a community with the expectation that our lives would be enriched by those around us, and that we would be part of the enrichment of others. This, of course, breaks down when there is no trust and when we operate on the basis of fear. Driven by fear we will always seek to be one jump ahead and will manipulate so that we are always in a position of advantage. The inevitable conflict is a disease which destroys rather than nurtures human relationships. The urge to dominate is deeply rooted.

Jesus tackled this fear head on. He presented a revolutionary approach to human relationships. He addressed this personal insecurity by giving us a radical new model. He spoke about denying self and of losing the self. He rejected all claims to privilege and status, redefining the notion of greatness. He called in question all structuring of society, church and family based on domination, power, or self-interest. The supreme symbol of Jesus' way of life is the Cross. He not only died on the Cross but lived out the Cross-life. The way of the Cross, the way of humility, submission and servanthood was, and is, the essence of his ministry. By being 'The Servant' he blazed a trail for all of us to follow in our relationships with others. Jesus summarized the whole law in two commandments to love. The first commandment is this: 'Hear, O Israel, the Lord our God is the only Lord. You shall love the Lord your God with all your heart, with all your soul, with all your mind, and with all your strength.' The second is this: 'Love your neighbour as yourself.' There is no other commandment greater than these. Love of God is primary, love for each other follows from that.

In our concern to be great we strive to keep the edge, to dominate, to be first. Jesus teaches us that true greatness is in servanthood. The pinnacle of human achievement is to love. He encourages us to face up to the fear of giving in to others by showing us that to serve is the mark of true greatness. In this also is freedom. When we choose to love others by serving them we experience true liberation. We are released from the awful burden of always needing to be right. We are given new joy in our ability to value other people, to express concern for their well-being and to put them first.

It has to be admitted that our fear that others will take advantage of us may well be justified. It is likely to happen.

But who can hurt someone who has freely chosen to love through servanthood? This is not a 'worm theology', a false attempt to devalue our own potential and gifts, but a deliberate choosing of the way of Christ. As such it is an agent of transformation, it becomes a point of growth, a threshold across which we step into new areas of freedom and joy.

On one occasion I was robing in a cathedral vestry preparing to take part in a service. A number of clergy were there, including an internationally known, and much loved, teacher and scholar. We were disturbed by a nervous and somewhat officious verger who had clearly come to get us organized. I felt irritated by the interruption, but will never forget the loving, gentle and courteous way the speaker responded. It taught me an important lesson. True greatness is not lost, rather it is enhanced, through servanthood.

In quite extraordinary ways Jesus turned things upside-down. He spoke of a Kingdom, not built on military might, but on mutual love and submission. He spoke of a way of life that had at its heart the challenge to deny ourselves. The power he spoke about was not power to dominate and repress, but the power to bring life and freedom. He commanded his followers, with some expectation of obedience, to love even their enemies. The Kingdom of Christ is radical and new. Within it, the law of love is to operate, not the law of the jungle.

One of the most disturbing paradoxes contained in Jesus' teaching is seen in his emphasis on the principle that the way to self-fulfilment is through self-denial. This, of course, does not come easy. Egalitarian values and a preoccupation with self have caused us to miss the point about servanthood. We find it hard to let go of our own desires and give way to others, and we find it unnatural to love our enemies. Everything within us shrieks out against the violation of our rights. We want to be known and valued as being strong, in control, on top. A life-style of servanthood which we imagine will threaten our security, even our identity, is almost unthinkable. But this is precisely what Jesus asked when he said, 'Whoever wants to become great among you must be your servant, and whoever wants to be first must be slave of all' (Mark 10:43–4). We shrink from this inversion of the natural order; nevertheless, we cannot escape the fact that our pilgrimage is a calling to be downwardly mobile.

I suggest that the graveyard in the margin of our minds is haunted by ghosts of fear. Fear of being devalued, fear of being despised, fear of being put down and marginalized, fear of being buried under an avalanche of rejection and disapproval, fear of being entombed in someone else's will. Above all, the fear of nothingness, of not mattering. Instead of confronting and exposing these fears we have fled from them down through the years until they have assumed massive proportions. The fears that drive us into selfism, that make us dominate and exploit others before they do the same to us, are like manacles that burden and bind us to a crippling way of life. We need Jesus to burst these chains of selfism. There is a way we can choose. The way of freedom is the way of Christ. Servanthood, not domination, will set us free. Martin Luther wrote, 'A Christian man is the most free lord of all, and subject to none; a Christian man is the most dutiful servant of all, and subject to everyone.' Thus, the paradox is captured, we are invited into a relationship with God, 'whose service is perfect freedom'. In divine captivity we are totally free.

I hope the reader can agree that much of life is spent in finding 'self', when Jesus calls us to lose 'self'. Much of our effort goes to justifying 'self', when Jesus calls us to give way. Much of our energy is spent in hating those who offend us, when Jesus calls us to love them. Much time is given to glorifying 'self', when Jesus bids us to deny 'self'. We seek to dominate others when Jesus calls us to serve. Many hidden fears, insecurities and anxieties build up in the subconscious mind that are to do with self-preservation. Jesus wants us to be free – the way to freedom is servanthood.

George Matheson's hymn speaks clearly:

Make me a captive, Lord,
And then I shall be free;
Force me to render up my sword,
And I shall conqueror be.
I sink in life's alarms,
When by myself I stand;
Imprison me within Thine arms,
And strong shall be my hand.

We are beckoned by God who invites us to step across the
threshold into a lifetime of servanthood. However, a caution
needs to be sounded. The movement from self-centredness to
servanthood is undoubtedly a decision, but is also a way of life.

The Process Begins

In developing this theme further I will use some illustrations
from the teachings of Jesus, some from my own experience,
but principally will base what I say on a book in the Old
Testament. Habakkuk is a little-known prophecy tucked away
in the Old Testament but it has great value to us because it
charts the process by which one man moves towards servanthood.

To my mind this book shows how God often takes the harsh
realities of life and uses them to soften a person, increase his
trust, and create within him a servant heart. Habakkuk agon-
izes over the discrepancy between his knowledge of God and
his experience. The veil is drawn back to reveal the painful
conflict that occurs when the prophet seeks to reconcile the
realities of life with the conviction that God is in control.
His is a world of ambiguities and contradictions. How can he
reconcile God's power and love with events that appear to deny
both? The process by which he comes to terms with this is one
whereby he is moulded and made more truly a servant of God
and a servant of God's people. This is the way of the Servant

Christ, who was obedient, even to death on a cross. It is, supremely, the Cross which holds together the contrast between the sovereignty of God and the tragedy of human experience. Thus servanthood was formed in Christ and will be formed also in us.

The Making of a Servant

Servanthood is the essence of Jesus' ministry. To model our lives on him brings us to the threshold of exciting new possibilities. We cannot, however, cross this threshold without pain and disturbance. Jesus challenges our view of ourselves and redirects us. In the process of transformation there will be much pain. In one of the most powerfully moving passages of the New Testament Jesus makes his point. He had gathered the disciples around him in the Upper Room for the Passover meal – to be called the Last Supper in Christian tradition. The disciples sat around, feet caked with dirt and sweat. Convention required that the least among them should perform the task of foot washing. No one moved. None of the disciples were sure that they could be the greatest, but none of them wanted to be the least.

Then occurred the moment that marked forever the character of Christ's ministry, and spelled out clearly the pattern he wished his disciples to follow. As the disciples watched with breathless amazement, Jesus took off his outer clothing, bound a towel round his waist, and washed their feet. The text says it all:

> Having loved his own who were in the world, he now showed them the full extent of his love . . . he got up from the meal, took off his outer clothing, and wrapped a towel round his waist. After that, he poured water into a basin and began to wash his disciples' feet, drying them with the towel that was wrapped around him. (John 13:1, 4–5)

The unfathomable love of God entered the superficial human world. This message is writ large on the personality, teaching and example of Jesus. He was the only one in the Upper Room who knew true freedom. The One who is called Lord of All has established an uncomfortable precedent. Our self-centred human nature may acknowledge the greatness of this act, but will find it hard to follow. If we follow it at all, we tend to be selective. Some feet we may wash, others we will not at any price. Jesus washed the feet of all the disciples, including the one who betrayed him, the one who doubted him, and the one who denied him. How can we who strain and strive for recognition and honour begin to understand this, let alone follow Christ's example?

My answer, drawn from years of experiencing and observing the way God deals with men and women, is that he has to initiate within us a process that compels us to acknowledge his authority and enables us to accept the way of the Cross.

The book of Habakkuk reveals one of God's methods (a common one) of doing this. It opens up the heart and inner conflict of a confused man who is trying to hang on to his belief in the sovereignty of God while surrounded by utter chaos. Put more simply it asks the question, 'how can I believe in a loving and powerful God when all the evidence seems to point to the fact that he is neither?' For Habakkuk the dilemma was caused by the grotesque spectacle of a heathen nation destroying, by cruel means, the people of God. For us, it might be the tragic death of a loved one, or the agonizing dilemma of mass starvation in a world of plenty. The text speaks:

> How long, O Lord, must I call for help,
>   but you do not listen?
> Or cry out to you, 'Violence!'
>   but you do not save?
> Why do you make me look at injustice?
>   Why do you tolerate wrong?
> Destruction and violence are before me;

there is strife, and conflict abounds.
Therefore the law is paralysed
    and justice never prevails.
The wicked hem in the righteous
    so that justice is perverted. (1:1–4)

There is an uncomfortably familiar ring about these questions. Why has this happened to me? Why don't you do something, Lord? Why do you tolerate evil and injustice in your world? Such questions form the common currency of people, who, in their relationship with God, wrestle daily with the paradoxes and contradictions that seem to be woven into human life. On the one hand we acknowledge the power of Almighty God, on the other we have to come to terms with apparent evidence of his impotence. As soon as we begin seriously to attend to this issue the process of moulding has begun.

I want to say something that I believe to be very important about the Bible. It refuses to be treated merely as a manual for personal salvation. One of the most significant things about the book of Habakkuk is that it forces us to look away from our own interests in order to acknowledge the community and world context in which we live. It pointedly challenges the self-centredness of much of our thinking and does so by making us wrestle with the ambiguities and contradictions of life. God erodes our smug certainties by making us face up to uncertainty. He challenges our views of our own greatness by presenting us with what appear to be challenges to his greatness. The path thus opened up becomes a path of transformation as we are changed from a narrow and exclusive self-interest to an awareness of the pain and misfortune of others. This is a threshold we must cross if life is to have meaning, and if we are in any sense to love and serve our fellow human beings.

When Habakkuk had the courage to ask the question 'Why?' his dilemma increased. Not only did God appear to delay a response to the prophet's cries for understanding, but also, when realization of the truth slowly began to dawn, it was

totally unacceptable. Habakkuk was faced with the ultimate
horror. God, whose eyes are too pure to look on evil and who
cannot tolerate wrong, was apparently doing both.

Habakkuk was told that a vicious and cruel nation, the Babylonians, whose name had become synonymous with all that was
worst in acts of barbarism, and who had scant regard for any
human life, was going to be used to punish his own nation.
This was unthinkable. 'Lord, you can't let this happen to me!'
This is a prayer which I think will find an echo in everyone's
heart.

Of all the experiences that can occur, it is in this particular
arena that our lives are turned inside out and in which a Christlike nature can be formed. Every experience we have, which
has the marks of the Cross about it, injustice, pain, desolation,
and rejection, could be the means by which the Christ-life is
formed in us.

Facing the Unacceptable

Anyone who thinks seriously about human nature and God's
dealings with humankind will have reflected on this question.
Why in the face of obvious evil and injustice does God seem
silent and inactive? The scope of this question can be vast,
ranging from world events to personal tragedies. Why did God
allow this to happen? Why did he not intervene? In considering
this I want to make what I think is an important observation.
The drive to have things our own way is checked when we have
to accept that God does not always fall in line with our will
and do things according to our understanding. God sometimes
has an uncomfortable way of answering our prayers, and frequently uses means other than those we expect or approve. An
elderly lady asked her vicar to pray that she might have more
patience. The vicar agreed and began, 'Lord, send thy servant
tribulation . . .' She stopped him in his prayer and demanded
to know why he prayed in that manner. He explained. 'You

know what the Scriptures say, don't you? ". . . tribulation worketh patience." ' She wanted a comfortable way of having her prayers answered. Faced with a dilemma or tragedy, our instinctive response is to do something that will bring a resolution. In any event, our activity occupies our minds and prevents us from learning all there is to learn from the situation. Waiting on God, bringing our doubts, fears, anger and frustration to him gives us time to have a clearer perspective, and opens the way for God to speak to us. There is a higher wisdom that we must engage. God sometimes appears not to act because he wants us to draw close to him and hear his word for ourselves. The sensations of personal impotence, of inability to influence affairs, are part of the moulding process.

When faced with tragedy in personal or world events the wise person listens to God and then speaks and acts. We will have far more to give to others in these circumstances than if we simply flooded each human dilemma with hastily conceived advice, or simply added to another's burdens by airing our pet theories. Depth, compassion, perception and understanding are required, such qualities are formed in the process of waiting on God. The prophet Habakkuk, like many since, felt that God was not listening.

The real problem occurred, however, when Habakkuk realized that God had heard and was about to act. The prophet was in danger of missing what God was doing for a very simple reason. He did not like what God said he would do. God's answer to Habakkuk's prayer was even more of a problem than his silence. Most of us have our own view about how God should answer our prayers, but what if the answer is unexpected, unacceptable?

'. . . I am going to do something in your days
    that you would not believe, even if you were told.
I am raising up the Babylonians,
    that ruthless and impetuous people,

who sweep across the whole earth
   to seize dwelling-places not their own.'

(Habakkuk 1:5,6)

This was a most shocking turn of events. Habakkuk was horrified at what God intended to do. He protests loudly:

Your eyes are too pure to look on evil;
   you cannot tolerate wrong.
Why then do you tolerate the treacherous?
Why are you silent while the wicked
   swallow up those more righteous than themselves?

(1:13)

These words also have a familiar contemporary ring about
them. There is more than a hint of desperation, of anger,
expressed by the prophet. Some friends of ours faced one of
the most painful human experiences imaginable. Their lovely
twenty-one year old daughter was dying of cancer. They
prayed, I prayed, the church prayed, yet she died. In one of
the most moving moments of my life I conducted her wedding
service in a hospital ward, attended by her family, close friends
and hospital staff. This girl, who had a great deal to live for,
died a month later in a local hospice. I remember being very
angry with God, searching for some meaning to the whole
situation. Slowly some important truths dawned on me as I
shared this time with her family. Supremely, I learned that it
is not the length of life that is all-important, but its quality, its
potential to touch others, and its ability to reveal the love of
God. This remarkable girl, even in the painful and confusing
process of dying, had about her a God-given love and quality
of life that affected deeply those with whom she came into
contact. Everyone who met her was immeasurably richer
because of her life.

   God can cope with, even expects, our anger when tragedy
touches our lives. However, it can be a growth point, a thres-

hold to cross, a moment of transformation as we move into new experiences of compassion and understanding. We are made softer, more usable, more approachable, and a means of infinite blessing to others. I once read that Stradivarius, the great violin maker, always chose wood from the north side of the tree. This was the part of the tree that stood facing the violent north winds, taking the full force of every storm. Wood from this part of the tree, he claimed, created instruments that played the sweetest music.

Our repeated acts of submission to God, especially when we do not understand, when all our instincts rebel, is the process by which we learn submission to others.

The Servant of God

For Habakkuk the softening process had begun. He received the courage to lay aside his own preferences and face up to his subsequent fears. The first step was a step of faith whereby he was enabled to trust God even though he could not understand. If he could allow God to do things his way there was every possibility that he could learn to quell his strident and indignant protests at the way life was turning out for him. The nursery in which we learn to curb the obsession with having our own way is in our relationship with God. As we can say 'Your will be done', so we become less anxious about insisting on our rights in human relationships. Submission to God comes first, submission to each other follows. A critical moment occurs in the movement from self-centredness to servanthood when we turn to face God.

Faced with an unbearable burden Habakkuk shouts at God and then turns to him for understanding. Speculation is at an end, he must have an answer.

> I will stand at my watch
>   and station myself on the ramparts;

> I will look to see what he will say to me,
>   and what answer I am to give to this complaint.
>
> (2:1)

Without ignoring the problems that faced him, the prophet turned his back on them and placed himself in the hands of God.

Faced with an unresolvable problem we need the humility to acknowledge we need God. Our striving for self-assertion, self-determination frequently distorts our perspective, making our judgements unreliable. We need God's perspective. Sometimes in the searching, in the 'not-knowing' God is to be found. Our spiritual sensitivities are developed, our appetite sharpened as we turn to him in the delays and frustrations of life. In the mystery of not-knowing, God gives us true knowledge. 'I will look to see what he will say to me.' The prophet is not disappointed. The Lord answers him: ' "Write down the revelation . . . For the revelation awaits an appointed time; it speaks of the end, and will not prove false. Though it linger wait for it . . ." ' (2:2,3). The answer is an invitation to trust. It is as though God is saying, 'I have heard your prayer, I understand your confusion, trust me and I will act.' It is enough for Habakkuk to know that the situation had not taken God by surprise. The movement across the threshold from disillusionment to trust is a crucial moment for the prophet.

There is something infinitely mysterious about the ways of God. Human wisdom is stood on its head as we confront tragedy and in the glimmerings of a new light begin to see God's purposes at work. The ultimate tragedy, the ultimate dereliction, the ultimate injustice was the Cross, but through it we experience the love of God in a unique way. The Cross stands forever at the threshold, spanning the gulf between human sin and new life.

In the dialogue with Habakkuk God reveals two very important truths. First, nothing can happen which is outside God's province. His glory covers the whole earth: 'For the earth will be filled with the knowledge of the glory of the Lord, as the waters cover the sea' (2:14). Second, God is still very much in control of events. 'But the Lord is in his holy temple, let all the earth be silent before him' (2:20).

The servant of God meets with God and falls into breathless, adoring silence. This silence is to be contrasted with the strident protestations of his earlier reactions and marks a transformation from emptiness and anxiety to fulness and peace. We frequently pray, 'For Thine is the Kingdom, the power and the glory', without knowing what we are affirming. Habakkuk helps us to clothe these words with understanding. The glory of God is the unmistakable, awe-inspiring, breath-taking, fearful presence of the living God. It is the unspoken, but overwhelming manifestation of God's holiness. It is a movement from chaos to order. The point at which we truly see the glory of God is the point at which our words of protestation dry up like spots of rain on a bonfire. The only appropriate response in the presence of God is the profound eternal silence of hearts adoring the Holy Mystery. The transformation from noisy self-justification to peaceful silence is complete. We dare not speak! We are unable to speak because of his presence, and we are unwilling to speak because, intuitively, we know that in the silence we will get understanding. The fear of the Lord is the beginning of wisdom.

It is there in the silence that we become whole. We are enthralled and satisfied in his presence. In this place conflicts are resolved, paradoxes revealed, and the dawn of enlightenment breaks.

As we see the greatness and glory of God, so a true perspective is given to our human problems. God touches us and sets us free, and in our hearts we know.

Servant of God's People

The movement continues, from servant, to servant of God, to servant of God's people. The passageway of transformation from selfism to true Christian love for others is through the Threshold God. He beckons us toward himself inviting our love and submission. Such a movement away from self makes it possible for us to love others, because the love of God is formed in us. The Christian understanding of love has been expressed in a rich tradition beginning with Jesus, and exemplified in the life and teaching of a remarkable variety of people down through the ages. All bear witness to the fact that the love of God improves and increases love for others. Luther wrote, 'a Christian man lives not in himself but in Christ and in his neighbour . . . He lives in Christ through faith, in his neighbour through love.'[1]

The revelation that was given to Habakkuk about the judgement of God contained the unpalatable truth that God was acting because of the sins of the people. God does not act capriciously or exercise correction for the sake of making life difficult. He acts always for a purpose, especially to confront and redress the waywardness of his people. Anti-religious prejudice may try to convince us that the concept of sin is outdated. Nevertheless, we are confronted at every turn by its devastating effect in the affairs of men and women. The Russian Christian, Alexander Solzhenitsyn, perceptively commented:

> Gradually it was disclosed to me that the line separating good and evil passes not through states, nor between classes, nor between political parties either – but right through every human heart . . .
>
> Since then I have come to understand the truth of all the religions of the world: they struggle with the evil inside a human being (inside every human being). It is impossible to

expel evil from the world in its entirety, but it is possible to constrict it within each person.

And since that time I have come to understand the false-hood of all revolutions in history: they destroy only those carriers of evil contemporary with them (and also out of haste, to discriminate the carriers of good as well). And they then take to themselves as their heritage the actual evil itself, magnified still more.[2]

The biblical view is that sin is located in the will of each one of us. It is something that all humans possess. Responsibility for its presence cannot altogether be transferred to environ-mental or hereditary factors, social conditions or other external realities. Nor can it be dismissed as a symptom of sickness in one form or another. Ordinary people make a choice, albeit under pressure from the subtle temptations of the evil within, to act in a manner which is at discord with the revealed will of God. Christians, frequently undefended by their own theo-logians, have been seduced towards the position that evil lies only, or primarily, in society. Individuals are consequently not to be held accountable.

However, the Song of Five Woes (Habakkuk 2:6–19) illus-trates the fundamental biblical principle that sin brings its own nemesis. In uttering judgement upon the sins of the Babyloni-ans the prophet acts as the spokesman of God declaring his attitude towards all those who break the law of love. Woe to him who takes by aggression what is not his. Woe to him who looks after his own interests, who feathers his nest at another's expense. Woe to him who takes pride in human achievements which have been accomplished by violent means. Woe to him who practises inhumanity, and cruelly destroys land, cities and people for their own base gain. The final woe is against idolatry, and addressed to those who 'make idols that cannot speak'. Self-love, whether blatantly flaunted or subtly disguised, has long been recognized as the source of idolatry.

'Of what value is an idol, since a man has carved it?
   Or an image that teaches lies?
For he who makes it trusts in his own creation;
   he makes idols that cannot speak.'

(2:18)

This forms a vital link with the thoughts presented in chapters 1 and 2. God is reduced to a form of self-projection. He is minimized, packaged and controlled, thus making him subject to our human will. One hideous result of this, of course, is that it enables us to side-step the most important challenge of Christianity – the decentring of the self.

Otto Baab, in his study of Old Testament theology, writes:

Idolatry is well understood in the Bible as differing from the pure worship of Israel's God in the fact of its personification and objectification of the human will in contrast with the superhuman transcendence of the true God. When an idol is worshipped, man is worshipping himself, his desires, his purposes and his will . . . As a consequence of this type of idolatry man was outrageously guilty of giving himself the status of God and of exalting his own will as of supreme worth.[3]

Habakkuk discovered, both for himself and the people of his time, that the pathway from self-love to servanthood was through the 'righteousness of faith', which took full account of God's holiness and his judgement against sin, especially sins against others. In this process the glimmerings of truth, which are to come to full brightness in the Cross, are to be seen. For us the Cross is the Threshold. A new life opens up enabling us to make the transformation from narcissistic self-love to love of neighbour, even love of our enemies. The Cross, the great act of Christ's submission, contains within it the seeds of all acts of submission to one another.

Habakkuk 3 is a majestic psalm of praise which captures not

only the prophet's trust in God, but also his total identification with the people. Not distanced from them, but part of them.

> Lord, I have heard of your fame;
>   I stand in awe of your deeds, O Lord.
> Renew them in our day,
>   in our time make them known;
>   in wrath remember mercy.

(3:1,2)

The prophet was reminded of the way God had spoken through his mighty acts of deliverance in the history of his people. He stood with the people and prayed for a renewal of God's deliverance and love for them. He had become the man for others.

The servant of God's people prays for a renewal of God's acts that will lead to a renewal of God's people. 'I have heard you', said the prophet, 'through recent events, through the history of your people, I stand in awe of your deeds – please do again in our time and for all of us, the great things you have done in the past.' Habakkuk stands with God's people as the mouthpiece of judgement, but also as judged with them. He did not seek merely to secure his own forgiveness, but brought the people to God. The true prophet/servant has a double courage. To speak the message and to share the blame. This has all the marks of the incarnation about it. We cannot distance ourselves from sinful humanity, nor from the sinful church. Christlike we must become servants of the people praying for their deliverance and spiritual renewal. The prophecy ends on a very poignant note:

> Though the fig-tree does not bud
>   and there are no grapes on the vines,
> though the olive crop fails
>   and the fields produce no food,
> though there are no sheep in the pen

> and no cattle in the stalls,
> yet I will rejoice in the Lord,
> I will be joyful in God my Saviour.
>
> (3:17,18)

Whatever the result, whatever the outcome I will still rejoice. At this point all thoughts of personal reputation, of having our own way, of pursuing a life of self-interest, recede dramatically into the background. The process of becoming the servant of others is the means whereby God addresses our need for status and domination and gives us the freedom to love. The Threshold God beckons us into a new Christ-life which celebrates the freedom that comes through servanthood.

4

Strength and Weakness

Experiences frequently occur that have some emotional component which lodges them in our memory. Mercifully, there are usually many happy incidents which cause us pleasure, but there are others, which, when recalled, flood us with shame and embarrassment. Sometimes I relive conversations I have had in the past when I have spoken carelessly or unwisely and caused other people pain. Occasionally, I learn important things about myself through these experiences, but also, I become more aware of the mass of complex emotions which exist just under the surface of human relationships. One can suddenly be launched into a situation in which a confusion of normal categories takes place.

One such memory, like Banquo's ghost, often comes back to haunt me. A very gifted Christian woman and I were having a discussion about a matter that was very important to both of us, and about which there was considerable disagreement. As the discussion developed and we both became more committed to pressing our points of view, the conversation became more and more heated until, to my shame, my friend burst into tears. She felt exasperated with herself for giving in to what she considered to be a weak response. I felt remorseful that I was the cause of her tears. I have no doubt that we were both unwise to allow the discussion to develop in this way, nevertheless, it gave me new insight into the conflict that exists within valued relationships. In the space of a few moments complex forces had surfaced which were an explosive mixture of fear, memory, hurt, insecurity, anxiety, pride and the like.

She had been taught that tears were a sign of weakness and kept apologizing for them while at the same time asking me to continue as if they had not happened. My reaction was to feel guilty and remorseful to the extent that I was ready to retreat from my position almost to the point of capitulation. Here were two people, normally regarded as strong, who were almost involuntarily displaying weak responses.

Tears serve many valuable functions as a normal safety valve for day-to-day stress, some would even describe them as a gift, and yet, located deep within our emotional folklore is the feeling that they are a demonstration of weakness. I can think of many other situations in which I have been faced with people who should give in to tears, but don't. Talking through the events surrounding the death of his wife an elderly man fought to keep back his tears. He continually apologized to me for displaying, what he obviously considered, a weakness. It is impossible to say who in particular was responsible for shaping this woman's and the old man's thinking about strength and weakness, but curiously both had got it wrong. My friend's tears were not necessarily a sign of weakness, any more than the old man's stoical resistance to them was a sign of strength. In human relationships many of us have a false view about strength and weakness.

The matter is further complicated because we not only have our own inner emotional landscape to become familiarized with, but we also have to cope with the considerable variations that arise through each new relationship as it changes the contours of that landscape. In relationships balances of power are established in which strong and weak responses are instinctively given. We are strong towards some and weak towards others. The thing is, however, that these responses are constantly shifting. There are many variables, to do with getting to know people better, to do with conscious and unconscious responses, and to do with the unique play-off between particular personalities.

Those who are weak may learn how to use their weakness

to dominate and control others. Incidentally, tears may be a weapon used to this end. Similarly, those who present themselves as being strong may have learned how to publicize their strengths in order to draw attention away from weaknesses they do not care to reveal.

The point is, appearances of strength and weakness have an element of illusion about them. The weak admire the strength of the strong, not seeing it as the smokescreen it is. The strong distance themselves from everyone because they fear exposure of their weaknesses. The question of dominance and submission, strength and weakness are implicitly present even in mutually peaceful relationships. This gives rise to the next question.

Who Are the Weak, Who the Strong?

I don't think it is an exaggeration to claim that most people for most of their lives will labour under the mistaken impression that there are two kinds of people, the strong and the weak. But is it helpful to talk in this way? Can we look at someone and say, 'she is strong' or at another and say, 'he is weak', as though that were an adequate description of their personalities? We may, of course, think in these categories, but in reality people are much more complex than that. We envy the strong and pity, even abuse, the weak. Our own strengths will tend to make us proud and our weaknesses afraid. Those who think of themselves as being weak will look on those they perceive to be strong and will regard them with a mixture of admiration and fear. Curiously, the strong are also marked by fear. Fear that others will get close enough to see that their strengths, as often as not, are a front, a device to prevent others from discovering their weaknesses. The strong learn by a multitude of subtle means to exploit the weaknesses of the weak and therefore, by contrast, perpetuate their own illusion of strength.

There are many factors which push people to conclusions about their strengths and weaknesses. Personality, looks, age, sex, achievements, qualifications, gifts, career, marriage, social status and the like; the list is endless. The reality is that we are all made of the same human clay. All of us are weak because we are all afraid. Those who appear strongest may, in some respects, be weakest of all, because of a basic dishonesty which prevents them from facing themselves as they truly are. They concentrate on presenting the illusion of strength. Even the most gifted, the most brilliant and self-assured have times of self-doubt, when in their heart of hearts they admit that out-ward appearance does not correspond to inner reality. In addition, the strong, like Samson, live with the fear that some-one may discover the secret of their strength and take it away from them. The intelligent fear a waning of their intellectual powers, the rich fear the destruction of their sources of wealth, the beautiful fear the onset of old age. There are knife-edge fears that create a personality disease in which suspicion, defensiveness and fear play a destructive role.

It may be possible to say that the weak are more honest than the strong, more ready to face reality and therefore closer to the threshold of personality wholeness and integration than the strong. Strengths can get in the way of self-knowledge, and what is worse, prevent us from knowing God. Assessed in biblical terms, it is the weak, who, conscious of their weakness, offer their weaknesses to God, and thereby experience a trans-formation of weakness into strength. The dialogue recorded by St Paul is revealing. Having pleaded with God about removing his own weakness, he continues, 'But he [God] said to me, "My grace is sufficient for you, for my power is made perfect in weakness." ' This led St Paul to the conclusion, 'For when I am weak, then I am strong' (2 Corinthians 12:9,10). I have met people who demonstrate this. People who, in human terms, live unenviable lives often marked by serious disability, yet nevertheless exude a rich peace. They have accepted what they are and who they are, and in their weakness the eternal strength of God is manifest. Our quality of life is formed and improved, not so much by building on perceived strength, but by recognizing the strength of transformed weakness. In writing this chapter I have found a book by Dr Paul Tournier called *The Strong and the Weak* helpful. In it he uses an interesting illustration.

> I am driving my car: if there are some pigeons on the road I have no need to brake; I know that fear is their safeguard, and that they will fly away just in time to avoid being run over. But if I see hens on the road I take care, for I know that fear makes them panic, so that they are liable to rush straight under the car wheels.[1]

We can conclude that definitions of human personality which include the concepts of strength and weakness may be misleading. What is really important is how we respond to our inner fear. Like the pigeon and the hen there are two possible reactions. One leads to pain and annihilation, to be defeated by our fear, the other causes us to rise above it.

Winning and Losing

Our superficial assessment of another's weakness or strength is frequently based on the image they present as being one of life's winners or one of its losers. If you have a social pedigree, or if you are a consultant surgeon, a lecturer, a teacher, or an MP, you are likely to be treated with greater respect, your views listened to more attentively, than if you were unemployed. This is a hard fact of life. The implicit assumptions being made are to do with status, achievement and position, all of which produce a certain kind of authority, and all of which are perceived to indicate worth.

Such assumptions, of course, are not concerned with deeper truths which may offer more accurate indicators as to the person's character. We get stuck on those things which are to do with what a person does, or has achieved, rather than what he or she is.

Stephen Verney perceptively states 'that the answer to the cry "Who am I?" is not "I am what I have", but, "I AM what I AM" '.[2]

A person may be a winner in terms of material success, but a loser in terms of all that makes life truly worthwhile. The words of Jesus are refreshingly clear, 'What good will it be for a man if he gains the whole world, yet forfeits his soul?' (Matthew 16:26). To bring this about there needs to be a transformation of the egocentric to the Christocentric, a movement from the 'I' to the eternal 'I AM'. To cross this threshold will require us to let go of all that we cling to which has sustained an image of strength and has bolstered up the 'I'. It will involve for us, as it did for St Paul, a relinquishing of the 'I' so that we can receive the 'I AM' as a free gift. It involves the discovering of the eternal strength in our weakness and vulnerability.

To develop this theme I want to look at four biblical personalities who demonstrate that outward appearances can be pitifully deceptive, and are therefore not an accurate indicator of who wins and who loses.

I give two examples of stereotypes of strength, and then two of weakness. We look first at one of the patriarchs, Abraham. He was a man of great faith and spirituality, a giant of a man through whom God said he would bless all the nations of the earth. So important was this man that God identified himself by his name, 'I am the God of Abraham'. With Abraham the plan of redemption begins. In truth he was the human founder of the Church, the recipient of God's covenant love. He was a man of immense courage, prepared to leave the security of his homeland and venture on a course of action towards an undisclosed destination. Abraham is a hero of the faith, a strong man, a winner if ever there was one. Known and honoured by countless generations as the 'Friend of God', he is rightly revered as a great example to follow.

We need say nothing more about the importance of this person, or of his massive spiritual significance for the whole people of God. An incident occurred, however, which showed Abraham in a different light.

Now there was a famine in the land, and Abram went down to Egypt to live there for a while because the famine was severe. As he was about to enter Egypt, he said to his wife Sarai, 'I know what a beautiful woman you are. When the Egyptians see you, they will say, "This is his wife". Then they will kill me but will let you live. Say you are my sister, so that I will be treated well for your sake and my life will be spared because of you.' (Genesis 12:10–13)

In an extraordinary act of cowardice, that most men would not for a moment consider, Abraham put his wife's life and honour at risk, so that he would be treated well and his life spared by Pharaoh. This dishonourable trade-off revealed the fact that Abraham had not yet faced his inner weaknesses. This strong man demonstrated an abject fear quite out of line with his image and reputation. In fact, this lack of moral fibre leading to other regrettable decisions was a continuing problem for Abraham, surfacing in other unwise decisions to do with Hagar and with Lot.

The truth is captured with precision by C. S. Lewis in *Prince Caspian*. ' "You come from the Lord Adam and the Lady Eve," said Aslan. "And that is both honour enough to erect the head of the poorest beggar, and shame enough to bow the shoulders of the greatest emperor on earth." '[3] Admitting fear and weakness does not detract from strength but enhances it.

Our next biblical figure is taken from the New Testament, and is the apostle Peter, considered by Christian tradition as the founder of the New Testament Church. Abraham and Peter have a lot in common. Peter towers over the spiritual landscape of the New Testament just as Abraham did in the Old. He was there more or less from the beginning and has an immense reputation for his power and spiritual energy in building the Church. He was a kingpin in the New Testament community, a man of extraordinary faith and conviction. Yet in an eerily similar incident, Peter put his safety and well-being first before any consideration of the truth. When he was identified as a follower of Jesus, Peter denied it. Admittedly, it was at a point where to confess Christ would have put his own life in danger. Nevertheless, it was a shameful act of cowardice. Despite his earlier protestations of loyalty even unto death, his denial became increasingly more crude and vehement. When accused for the third time that he was a follower of Jesus, 'He began to call down curses on himself, and swore to them, "I don't know this man you're talking about" ' (Mark 14:71). The strong man displayed a pathetic, if understandable, weakness which we know he later regretted. This inability to stand firm for the truth in the face of opposition surfaced on other occasions and was no doubt a continuing source of humiliation to this great man. Like Abraham he had not yet experienced the transformation of the 'I' into the 'I AM'. True strength, as Peter's life indicates, is in having the courage to face the inner realities of our lives, it is to do with self-knowledge and it is to do with crossing the threshold of human weakness with God's strength. Abraham and Peter are both crucial figures who, in the history of the Church, are seen as strong because of our simplistic stereotypes. In fact, they are a mixture from which their unique roles originate.

We have looked at two men who appeared strong yet had not had the courage to face up to their weaknesses. We look now at the other side of the coin, at two people who are presented as weak but discovered, through their relationship with Christ, extraordinary inner strength.

Jesus told a parable concerning a Pharisee and a tax collector who both went to the temple to pray. The Pharisee recited a fairly impressive list of his law-keeping and good behaviour, the tax collector, on the other hand, '. . . stood at a distance. He would not even look up to heaven, but beat his breast and said, "God, have mercy on me, a sinner" ' (Luke 18:13). The Pharisee, one of life's winners, was incapable of speaking with honesty about himself. The tax collector, a despised person, a nobody, had the courage to face his inner condition and ask God for mercy. This is a sign of true strength. No pretence, no self-justification, but a simple admission and plea for mercy. The tax collector, a loser in every sense of the word, by an act of courageous self-assessment and humility, placed himself in the gallery of the great. The Pharisee, on the other hand, impressed only himself. The tax collector has left an outstanding example to follow. He did something that has echoed down the years as a compelling model of discipleship. The Pharisee remained locked in his prison, the tax collector crossed the threshold into true freedom. Jesus told this parable to subvert notions of strength and weakness. One character defines himself by what he is not (others), the other by what he is (a sinner). John Baillie wrote, 'Humility is the obverse side of confidence in God, whereas pride is the obverse side of confidence in self.'

The other person I want to mention I have already referred to in chapter 1. Mary Magdalene, the woman who anointed Jesus with perfume. For the purposes of this book I follow the tradition which identifies this unnamed woman as Mary Magdalene. Mary is a hidden figure emerging from time to time out of the background of the New Testament. When Matthew speaks of her breaking the jar of precious perfume and pouring it over Jesus he says that Jesus spoke movingly about this beautiful act. 'Wherever this gospel is preached throughout the world, what she has done will also be told, in memory of her' (Matthew 26:13). Mary's unselfconscious act of love has captured the imagination of people for almost two thousand years, though if she was being assessed professionally today she would almost certainly be labelled an hysterical personality, a 'wandering womb', a woman with a morass of sexual frustrations. Even in the Gospels she is seen to be a problem,

being identified with a particular form of weakness and broken-
ness. Very much a loser.

In an act of great generosity and extravagant earthy affection,
she approached Jesus to anoint him with perfume. The disciples
obviously resented this act and dismissed it as inappropriate.
Mary demonstrated a double courage. She 'wasted' something
of great financial value, but also made herself utterly vulnerable. In a society where reason, because of her background,
would compel her to conform in order to earn approval, she
made a refreshingly disorderly, spontaneous gesture of passion.
As far as the observers were concerned, it was uncomfortably
in tune with her previous life-style. Her gesture earned censure
from the disciples, acceptance from Jesus, and from the readers
of Christian history: admiration. 'She has done a beautiful thing
to me', said Jesus. This is also the verdict of history.

This extravagant passion is at the heart of true human courage. It is a strong response from someone regarded by her
contemporaries as weak and it earned Mary a place in the
history of the Church as an exemplar of true love. Jesus used
her action to redefine the nature of strength and weakness.

Mary Magdalene, far more than some of the better known
personalities of the New Testament, blazed a courageous trail
across the threshold of acceptable norms of behaviour into the
spiritual history of the world and into the carefree joyfulness
of God's love. Commenting on this incident Père de la Columbière said: 'It is certain that of all those present the one who
most honours the Lord is the sinner who is so persuaded of the
infinite mercy of God that all her sins appear to her as but an
atom in the presence of His mercy.'[4]

Who are the winners and losers of this life? This question
needs careful reflection. The Bible presents us with some astonishing surprises that challenge us right at the heart of our
humanness and calls in question our standard procedures for
establishing human worth.

The Great Paradox

In our search for God we stumble occasionally into profoundly important truths. Such a truth, as we have seen, is revealed by St Paul in these words.

> To keep me from becoming conceited because of these sur-passingly great revelations, there was given me a thorn in my flesh, a messenger of Satan, to torment me. Three times I pleaded with the Lord to take it away from me. But he said to me, 'My grace is sufficient for you, for my power is made perfect in weakness.' Therefore I will boast all the more gladly about my weaknesses, so that Christ's power may rest on me. That is why, for Christ's sake, I delight in weaknesses, in insults, in hardships, in persecutions, in difficulties. For when I am weak, then I am strong. (2 Corinthians 12:7–10)

When I am weak then I am strong. From a man universally regarded as strong there comes an arresting statement of a theology of weakness. Human weakness, rather than strength, is the means God uses to accomplish his purposes. The implications of such a theology of weakness are startling. God turns our worldly understanding upside-down. Robert Girard says, 'In God's topsy-turvy approach to power, he takes weak, scarred, scared, struggling, failing and ineffective people and accomplishes his mighty work with such miserably inadequate tools.'[5]

Christ's earthly life began in weakness and ended in weakness. The significance of this must not be missed. The helplessness of God is a very important truth. In our attempts to follow Christ we contrive models, based on flair, gifting and demonstrations of human strength. We impose what we think of as attractive onto the personality of Christ. The 'Rambo-Christ' of contemporary Christian triumphalist writings is as far removed from reality as the 'gentle Jesus meek and mild' of our Victorian forefathers.

An unfortunate consequence of current trends is that in order to establish credibility we ape the skills of the humanly strong and present this strength as a virtue. As a result we thrust Christians into years of heart-breaking frenetic activity. Only God has inexhaustible strength. He waits patiently for us to admit our weaknesses and then flows through us in a great surge of healing love. Henri Nouwen perceptively comments,

> There are many people who, through long training, have reached a high level of competence in terms of the understanding of human behaviour, but few who are willing to lay down their own lives for others and make their weakness a source of creativity. For many individuals, professional training means power. But the minister, who takes off his clothes to wash the feet of his friends, is powerless and his training and formation are meant to enable him to face his own weakness without fear and make it available to others. It is exactly this creative weakness that gives the ministry its momentum.[6]

I am no geologist, but as far as I understand it, the great rivers of our planet were formed as the waters of heaven and the great hidden deep found the weakest route along which to flow in the earth's crust. This meandering weakness gives the river maximum scope for its relentlessly surging life to bring fruitfulness to the land. The fault along which the river flows becomes part of the beauty of the landscape.

We can be so ashamed of our failures and weaknesses and, because of the desire to appear strong, cloak them so that no one, not even God, can see. True liberation and wholeness can begin to come as we yield those weaknesses to God to become instruments of life. This story is told of Martin Luther and his friend Philip Melanchthon, author of the Augsberg Confession. Melanchthon was a cool man where Luther was fervid, a scholar as opposed to a doer, who continued to live like a monk even after he had thrown in his lot with the German Reformation. One day Luther lost patience with Melanchthon's virtuous reserve. 'For heaven's sake', he roared, 'why don't you go out and sin a little? God deserves to have something to forgive you for.'

In truth, it is often our human strengths of which we should be most ashamed, for they keep us from God. If we would know true strength we must know God. His strength is made available through our weakness. Power through powerlessness is an important biblical theme. The very things that cause us most shame and fear are to be the means of infinite blessing to others. This is an important threshold to cross. Many get stuck in the doorway, trapped there by the baggage of all we have learned about human achievement and earthly power. We are afraid to shrug it off our shoulders, to be released of its burden because so much personal security is invested in it. Our human nature panics and screams out against this violation of natural law. Yet we are called on through the doorway, across the threshold into a new dimension. The exciting thing is surely this, that such a life is accessible to all, because all are weak. All of us experience weakness, and most live in fear that with the onset of age, our weaknesses increase. With such a theology of weakness old age, with all its accepted handicaps and limitations, can nevertheless open up remarkable new opportunities of joyful service in God's strength.

In human terms one frequently gets the impression that the older one becomes, the more of a nuisance, and consequently the more overlooked. In God's terms the older one becomes, the more valued and treasured. People do not retire from discipleship and Christian ministry. The day to day outworkings necessarily adjust, but the experience, wisdom and love of those who have lived longest become an appreciating asset to the Church. The outer journey may slow down but the inner journey quickens, keeping pace with the adventurous Spirit of God. It is upon human weakness, not human strength, that

God builds his most enduring work. He uses us, not in spite of our ordinariness and helplessness, but precisely because of them.

The Strength of God

'Lord, give me strength' is a common enough prayer, occasionally heard on someone's lips as an exclamation, but more often than not expressing a deep-seated instinct that mortals need help from a source outside of themselves. Let me make it clear that we are not talking about the false strength of someone who uses God as a means of dominating others. We are not talking, either, of those who are often acclaimed as strong but who crudely present themselves as the interpreters of God's will in order to manipulate others. Nor are we concerned with the common politics of human relationships which create a market in which people strive for the best deal. We are talking of a discovery of inner strength stemming from an experience of the living God. Such an encounter acts at a different level. It is not concerned with power relationships, but with changing human nature. And by changing human nature the whole arena of human relationships is significantly altered.

It is the strength that God gives which enables us to face the wilderness within. It is his strength which breaks the habitual power of our natural reactions. It is his strength which moves the centre of self from 'I' to 'I AM'. It is the strength of faith which conquers and overcomes fear. There are many exhortations in the Bible to be strong, but we must recognize that the faith is given whereby we can be strong. Exhorting a weak person to be strong would be cruel, unless he is given a new perspective of himself in relation to his problems. Such a perspective is given when we place ourselves in Christ and move across the threshold from the 'I' to the 'I AM'. 'I am with you, be strong', God says through the prophet Haggai. 'The joy of the Lord is your strength', proclaims Nehemiah. 'I love you, O Lord my strength,' declares the Psalmist who sees in God strength personified. 'Fear not', says Jesus over and over again in an attempt to point us away from our problems to faith in God. Our strength is in the fact that Christ indwells us. The One who is strength is our companion, helper and friend. He is our strong deliverer. The strength of God enables us to face our own inner wilderness with courage. The biblical examples I have used are increasingly explicit about the nature of strength. I now use a modern example which demonstrates true strength with stark clarity. I would like to tell the story of a friend of mine who wrote to me in an attempt to explain how God had given her strength to face her problems. The story is best told in her own words.

'This will not be easy to write nor, I fear, easy to read but I feel that you must understand more of the isolation of my past to appreciate the fulness of the new life I now have and the measure of healing I have experienced. I was sexually abused consistently from my infancy until I was married when I was twenty-two years old. From the age of eleven, two men were abusing me. The fear and horror I experienced undoubtedly took their toll but it is the side-effects that caused me the most pain. In both cases the men showed me a great deal of love and told me I was special. This was reinforced by my family. My mother never understood why I didn't want to be left alone with my uncle, why I didn't like playing piano duets with him, or putting the car in the garage or going on outings with him. She told me I was ungrateful for his love and concern for me. It never once occurred to me to tell her why I was frightened of him.

'As a child I felt that the problem was entirely of my own making and I was worried because I couldn't respond to loving gestures. This spilled over into my relationship with my father. I never wanted him to touch me or see me in bed. I always felt very guilty at my lack of response towards him. I knew that other children loved their fathers and my guilt was profound.

'There was an occasion when I was alone with the second

man who had been introduced to the family as an in-law, when I realized by the words he used and the gestures he made that he too was going to abuse me. At this point I was totally helpless to control my destiny and, dating from this moment, I began a pattern of behaviour which stayed with me up to age thirty-five. I began abusing my own body in the hope that I would be extricated from the situations I couldn't control.'

This moving and distressing letter went on for many pages in similar vein telling about the isolation, depression and confusion that resulted from her childhood experiences. It also told of the sexual problems which inevitably occurred with her marriage and of the feelings of increasing desperation and isolation. She talked of the overwhelming despair she experienced when she began to hit her children.

The turning-point came when a leader from her church insisted that she sought help. That help came in the form of a loving, patient husband, a perceptive GP, a skilled psychiatrist and a supportive church. There followed two years of painful and exhaustive work with the psychiatrist unravelling the tangled mess, but she was reassured by a picture given by a member of the church. Her letter continues.

'Right at the start of the two years of appointments the Lord entered into events with a calm reassurance that all was going according to his plan. He gave someone a picture for me of a tangled mass of roots out of which was growing a straight, strong green stem which was me. A month or so previously I had come across such a tangled mass of roots in my bag of potting compost and having recovered from thinking it was a mass of worms I remembered that it was a lily which had bloomed the previous year. I had repotted it and by the time the word was given to me it had grown the strong green stem and was there in my kitchen for many weeks reminding me that out of this wilderness I was going to be strong and new.'

Her letter continues to speak of the trauma of working through her feelings but ended with a note of confidence. There was yet more to do but she knew that God had taken away the guilt of the past and given her a new perspective in which she could face future relationships. This story points to the source of true strength. It does so without sentimentality, and without making false claims. I can verify the reality of all that has happened and am grateful for the insights her bravery has given me.

Change is a process requiring great courage. Faith does not do away with problems or necessarily replace our natural temperament, but by faith we are helped to change what must be changed. What Pascal says is always true: 'Banish what is natural and it comes running back.' Faith does not replace human nature, but ennobles and transforms it.

My friend has, in the strength of God, begun the process of transformation. However, for her, and for us all, that is the work of a lifetime. The truly strong are those who are prepared to face up to the inner reality and stay with it as the Holy Spirit brings transformation and wholeness. Such strength will hold together the work of the Spirit with the reality of life as it is. There will be no need for pretence. Henri Nouwen writes,

> The real spiritual guide is the one who, instead of advising us what to do or to whom to go, offers us a chance to stay alone and take the risk of entering into our own experience. He makes us see that pouring little bits of water on our dry land does not help, but that we will find a living well if we reach deep enough under the surface of our complaints.[7]

The Void of Loneliness

Loneliness terrifies us. Most of us fill up our time and keep busy because we are afraid of being alone. Without something to occupy our minds the jumbled, disturbing, thoughts and fears of a lifetime surge into the forefront, reminding us that the things we have refused to face are still there waiting for attention. We seek distraction in work, noise, company, leisure, alcohol; anything to anaesthetize us from our painful loneliness and fill the frightening void within.

The story is told about a clergyman who went to see Jung. He was a driven man, working fourteen hours a day, his ragged nerves bringing him to breaking-point. Jung began by asking him if he wanted to get well. Indignantly, the minister replied that obviously he did, otherwise he would not be there. Jung then gave him a very simple prescription. He was to work eight hours a day and sleep eight. The remaining hours he was to spend totally alone in his study, in complete silence. This seemed an easy solution, so he agreed to try it out. That day the clergyman worked only eight hours. At supper he explained to his wife what he was going to do, went into his study closing the door behind him determined to stay for several hours. He played some music and read a novel. Next day he followed the same routine, reading and listening to music in his study. The following day he went back to see Jung complaining that he felt no better. Jung asked what had happened and then said, 'I did not want you with a novel or with music, I wanted you to be all alone with yourself.' At this the minister looked horrified and said, 'Oh, but I can't think of any worse company.' To this Jung replied, 'And yet this is the self you inflict on other people fourteen hours a day.'

The truth is that many of us are running away from ourselves. Our loneliness is a symbol of self-hatred. We do not stop to think because we are afraid of what will be revealed about ourselves. What strange love we have for those closest to us if we inflict on them the company we cannot ourselves abide! The yawning chasm within us is too painful to enter, because in it we glimpse the disturbed, distorted images accumulated during a lifetime. We want something, or someone else to take away our pain. Loneliness is ultimately a refusal to face our inner life.

The Ache of Loneliness

Loneliness, as a factor of human experience, is by and large considered negatively. Loneliness equals unhappiness; this is the simple equation most people make. It is perceived as a problem to be dealt with, a sickness to be cured, a condition to be reversed. However, looked at from both a biblical and personal perspective, being alone has a very positive, health-giving potential. Part of the problem is vocabulary. We are used to people talking of their loneliness and almost always associating it with distress and unhappiness. I want to suggest that the experience of loneliness is an indicator that we need to face up to our inner life. Viewed this way, loneliness, instead of being an empty, sickening pit of disturbed emotions, can become a threshold, or passageway, leading to new understanding and peace.

In a study of loneliness, Rubin Gotesky distinguishes between aloneness, loneliness and solitude.[1] Aloneness denotes a simple spatial separation from other people which, in terms of feeling, is neutral. Loneliness, on the other hand, is a painful experience, the feelings we have when we are rejected or excluded. Solitude, however, is the state of being alone, and of being peaceful.

Confusion arises because we tend to lump all our experiences of aloneness under the single description 'loneliness', which encourages a negative interpretation. In fact, being alone is a necessary and desirable human experience, highly prized as a vital spiritual discipline. Jesus frequently sought to be alone. Some writers on this subject use the word 'solitude' to denote a positive condition, which needs to be distinguished from the more negative images conjured up by the word 'loneliness'. We can therefore talk of the transformation of loneliness, a quality of life to be feared, into solitude, a quality of life to be sought. Loneliness is an immense barrier to inner peace, but faced and entered it can be transformed into a passageway leading to a new understanding of ourselves.

Many people talk of their loneliness as being very unpleasant without being able to put a finger accurately on its cause. One friend of mine described it in terms of isolation. She felt secure when someone else knew her movements on a day to day basis, and would therefore be aware if she was ill. That someone was familiar with her routine was important to her. She spoke of her fear of returning from holiday and no one knowing of her arrival.

Others describe loneliness in terms of incompleteness, of feeling restless, frustrated, dissatisfied, discontent. For many people it is an indefinable longing, perhaps for love, for meaning, and for purpose in life. It is a bitter-sweet experience, being awakened with an aching longing to all that is possible, but continually finding it is just out of reach.

Sometimes this longing is focused on a person. Other times we experience it as an exposure to things that cannot be attained. Dreaming of the perfect marriage, the perfect job, the perfect life-style, contributes to our sense of loneliness because we are tantalized by the unobtainable. Rather than accept what we have, we want more, we want better, thus perpetuating the quest for the unachievable. Not surprisingly this quest becomes a habit, the real object forgotten, shifting from one person or thing to another. Its only legacy is a longing that cannot be satisfied, a restlessness that cannot be quietened, an aching that cannot be eased. Shakespeare wrote of 'immortal longings', as though the human spirit finds it impossible to be tranquil and satisfied with its lot.

We spend most of our lives, said Evelyn Underhill, conjugating three verbs, 'to want', 'to have', 'to do'. But none of these verbs has any ultimate significance until it is transcended by and included in the fundamental verb 'to be'. Successive generations have produced a society which measures a person's worth by success. The survival of the fittest is the implicit maxim of politicians, educationalists and sometimes even the church. Life is seen as competition, rarely as co-operation. Dr Paul Tournier speaks of the 'parliamentary spirit' that afflicts human nature and which sees life as a battleground. 'Hence it is that modern man, misled by nineteenth-century science and philosophy, can conceive of society only as a vast network of battles, tests of strength, and competition between rival powers.'[2]

With this perceived need to be strong, to keep on top, no one feels free to admit that they have any problems, in case such knowledge is used to gain advantage. This leads to a dissociation between the function and the person, with people increasingly keeping their private lives to themselves. A consequence of this is that people struggle alone with their temptations, problems and guilty fears, thus increasing their sense of personal loneliness. For many of us therefore loneliness is experienced as an insatiable longing for love, to know and be known as a person, not as a function. Our relationships are so fraught with incompleteness and conflict that we long for 'soulmates', people with whom we can share ourselves.

In describing their loneliness people talk of friendlessness, rootlessness, restlessness, and would hint at the meaninglessness of their lives. They feel they are living at the margin and have a vague sense that they are missing out on what life is all about. But this vacuum can be seen in positive terms.

Our experiences of aching loneliness are symptoms of a search for significance, a quest for being. St Augustine sums up this condition in his now famous words, 'Thou has created us for thyself, and our heart knows no rest, until it may repose in thee.'[3]

The Gift of Solitude

If loneliness is an experience people fear and run from, solitude is a gift to be received with joy. Loneliness is inner desolation, solitude is inner consolation. Many feel loneliness is something thrust upon them, solitude is something to be sought.

Jesus, in his earthly ministry, sought solitude. He began his ministry with forty days and nights in the wilderness. Frequently he returned to the hills alone to spend time with his Father. Obviously, we recognize that much of his time was spent with others because that was what he wanted, but we must also recognize that he needed solitude. In order to serve others we need to know how to be alone. Dietrich Bonhoeffer wrote about the balance that is necessary,

Let him who cannot be alone beware of community . . . Let him who is not in community beware of being alone . . . Each by itself has profound pitfalls and perils. One who wants fellowship without solitude plunges into the void of words and feelings, and one who seeks solitude without fellowship perishes in the abyss of vanity, self-infatuation, and despair.[4]

There is a paradox here that must be acknowledged. We are called into community, into families, and into relationships where so much is given and learned, yet we cannot be truly whole until we have learned the value of solitude. So much suffering is caused because we launch ourselves into relationships in the expectation that someone else will take our loneliness away. We invest other people with the almost Messianic hope that they will be the answer to our problems. I have met people who, lacking intimacy and affection in their immediate family circle, launch themselves prematurely into marriage and begin to produce children in the desperate hope that now at last they will have someone who will love them.

Pornography is a symptom of loneliness. What is it other than intimacy for sale? Men striving with pitiful desperation to enter into mental and emotional intimacy with glossy, untouchable, too-perfect women, in the pathetic hope that this will cause their loneliness to melt away. No friend, wife or lover, no community or social circle will be entirely able to still our restless longing. Many marriages are destroyed because the expectation of one partner that the other would take away their loneliness is not fulfilled. By burdening others with impossible expectations we simply alienate ourselves even further, creating in our friends feelings of inadequacy and helplessness when faced with our needs. The only response possible is for them to distance themselves from us in order to preserve their own identities. This clearly heightens our sense of loneliness.

Those who want to enter into marriage and into other close relationships must first have the courage to face their own loneliness. Love cannot develop if it is triggered primarily by an anxiety about being alone, because it will constantly claw and grasp to fulfil its own needs. This is not only destructive it is also deceitful. It is deceitful because it persuades us that when we have worn out one marriage or friendship, we can go on to another in the hope that this time our problems will be solved. This is a sad and pitiful state of affairs because, until we have faced up to ourselves, we are preconditioned to repeat all the mistakes of the past. Kahlil Gibran puts this beautifully in a poem on marriage:

> Sing and dance together and be joyous,
> but let each one of you be alone,

Even as the strings of a lute are alone though they quiver
   with the same music.
Give your hearts, but not into each other's keeping.
For only the hand of Life can contain your hearts.
And stand together yet not too near together:
For the pillars of the temple stand apart,
And the oak tree and the cypress grow not in each other's
   shadow.[5]

We need each other but, in order not to stifle love, there
must also be the ability to be alone. The chains of love must
hang loose or they will choke the life out of our relationships.
   In choosing solitude the first barrier to overcome is fear. To
be completely alone without noise or distraction renders us
vulnerable to a surging tide of thoughts we have so far kept at
bay by our busyness. Many seem to have a romantic image of
the spiritual disciplines, which produces a belief that the mere
act of sitting alone, or going for a quiet walk in the woods, will
produce tranquillity. This, as those who try it know, can be far
from the case. I will do anything to put off the moment when
I have to face up to myself and to God in solitude. Sitting
down to begin I will think of one more telephone call I must
make, one more conversation I must have, one more chore I
must do, and then I'll go and make another cup of coffee. The
time of quiet I had planned is soon eroded by a restless suc-
cession of inconsequential activity. Why does this happen? I
am afraid to face myself, afraid to listen to God speaking about
my life, afraid of the consequences of thinking thoughts I have
avoided for years. Like many other people I would do anything
to have a serene tranquil life; except the very thing that will
produce it. Perhaps the first step in overcoming this fear is to
acknowledge that the journey inward is a voyage of discovery,
not a dead end. There is rich hidden treasure in all of us that
can be unearthed in solitude. Above all, it is there, as we have
the courage to face the fear of being alone, that we meet with

God. Teresa of Avila rightly said, 'Settle yourself in solitude and you will come upon him in yourself.'

The prophet Elijah experienced this. Despite all he had done successfully to accomplish God's will he is found running away in a state of deep depression, both from his problems and from God. In a very moving account of the story recorded in 1 Kings 19, we see how God brought him to the place where he had to face up to things. God met with him and spoke to him, not in the powerful wind, nor in the shattering earthquake, nor in the searing fire, but in the sound of a gentle whisper.

The Need for Inner Silence

Dag Hammarskjöld, a former Secretary General to the United Nations, wrote, 'The best and most wonderful thing that can happen to you in this life, is that you should be silent and let God work and speak.'[6] But let's be honest, silence is difficult to cope with. For the past few years our family holiday has partly consisted of a period of time in a log cabin in the Scottish Borders, miles from any other human habitation. The cabin does not have electricity, so there is no telephone. It takes us a while to adjust to the profound silence of this place. For a while I feel restless, and a bit disorientated, until my mind begins to settle into the natural rhythm of the place. Experiencing withdrawal symptoms, I have a strong temptation to fill the silence by playing the radio more or less non-stop.

In order to create solitude there is the need for some form of withdrawal. A place where silence is possible is obviously desirable, but silence is not merely the absence of noise, it involves listening. What is important is an inner silence which can be achieved even when surrounded by noise. Catherine de Hueck Doherty wrote,

A day filled with noise and voices can be a day of silence, if the noises become for us the echo of the presence of God, if the voices are, for us, messages and solicitations of God. When we speak of ourselves and are filled with ourselves, we leave silence behind. When we repeat the intimate words of God that he has left within us, our silence remains intact.[7]

All the great masters of the spiritual disciplines would encourage us to find a place where silence is possible, but would also encourage us to find silence within the noise around us. It is the silence of the heart that is important. This inner silence, in which we can listen to God, is possible in the busiest life and can be found in the noisiest environment. Being aware of the momentary solitudes that occur during the normal day, and consciously using them as an offering to God is one way of beginning. Such moments according to T. S. Eliot are a 'still point in a turning world'. According to Thomas Merton they are 'contemplation in a world of action'. The creative use of these moments can begin to build within us an inner silence in which we can hear God. Of course, longer times alone with God are important, but God does not need two hours in order to speak within us. Like any human relationship, our relationship with God can be enriched by a multitude of moments of contemplation, attention and listening. So much time each day is frittered aimlessly away, we will be surprised at how significant the redemption of the odd moments can be. This point is made with stark but valid perception by Thomas à Kempis, in *The Imitation of Christ*: 'If you avoid unnecessary talk and aimless visits, listening to news and gossip, you will find plenty of suitable time to spend in meditation on holy things.'[8]

One could go further. Simply by taking the common events of everyday life and using them as an offering of love to God, this inner stillness and richness can be developed. One of the greatest spiritual treasures of the Western Church is a book called *The Practice of the Presence of God* written by Brother Lawrence, a seventeenth-century Carmelite lay brother and mystic. In his book Brother Lawrence tells of how he would try to make the least thought or the meanest task an offering in the presence of Jesus, even to picking up straw from the scullery floor as he went about his job of cleaning up after others.

In seeking to develop inner silence, or any other spiritual discipline, it is important not to overreach ourselves. We can be so challenged by this ideal of spirituality that we begin by taking too much on too soon.

It is helpful to begin, like Brother Lawrence, by transforming the most immediate and accessible areas of our lives. Just outside the study window of our previous home there was a small patch of garden enclosed by high walls. A blackberry bush grew around the base of two young apple trees, but was also intertwined with a rose bush. It was my job to pick the blackberries. One day, seeing a cluster of large blackberries in the centre of this tangle I carefully worked my way into the bushes. Restricted space meant that movement was difficult and likely to be painful because of the briars and thorns. Reaching out for the fruit I decided to go for the largest blackberries, which were also furthest away. In so doing I knocked the cluster closest to me, dislodging the fruit which fell to the ground out of reach. The exertion of stretching to the furthest point made me grasp the largest blackberry too roughly with the result it was crushed. All in all a wasted effort.

In developing our spiritual lives we can try too hard, reaching too far, and thus spoiling what may be within our reach. This danger is captured brilliantly by Adrian Plass, the Sacred Diarist:

Alarm clock exploded dead on 5.30 a.m. Crawled downstairs and knelt, bleary eyed, in the sitting room. Put my watch on the floor in front of me so as not to carry on past seven thirty.

Started contemplating eternity (the object of the exercise) at exactly 5.34 a.m.

Kept my eyes shut and tried to concentrate on things going on for ever and ever. Not easy. Found my thoughts drifting off to holidays and why you don't see those wicker paper baskets any more, and what a cross between a ferret and a giraffe could possibly look like. Was just imagining a creature with a ferret's body, and a neck so long that it could put its head right down a rabbit hole without moving its legs, when I remembered what I was supposed to be thinking about. Clenched my mind and really tried hard. After about an hour, opened my eyes to check the time. It was 5.44 a.m.

Thought about eternity for another couple of minutes, but my head began to ache. Tried going back to bed but I couldn't sleep.[9]

It is much better to begin with five minutes and build up from there, than attempt a discipline that cannot possibly be maintained. The key to successful spiritual growth is that we take the next step from where we are now. I will seek to develop this theme more fully in the next chapter.

6

The Journey in God

Frances de Sales said, 'After the journey to God, there is a journey in God.' No such journey can be undertaken however unless we practise the quality of inner silence. When we are seeking to develop disciplines that are not natural to us we obviously learn best when we have access to other people's experience. We know from the New Testament that Jesus placed a high priority on solitude and prayer but we are not told how he set about it. The assumption is frequently made that inner silence might have been easier to achieve in first-century Palestine because of the simple, less technological life-style of those times. After all, they did not have traffic noise or ghetto blasters or Walkmans. Wall-to-wall sound is a charac-teristic of the twentieth century. However, I'm not so sure that the issue is one of external distraction, it is much more to do with the restlessness of heart that has always characterized human nature.

Most profound truths are usually simply stated.

> Muddy water
> let stand,
> becomes clear

This was written by Lao Tse, a Chinese philosopher, five cen-turies before Christ, and indicates that we are not dealing with a modern phenomenon. Inner unrest and turmoil are part of what it is to be human, and each generation must apply its wisdom to resolve it. I suspect that the encouragement of inner

silence is neither easier nor more difficult in the twentieth
century than in the first century.

Everyone I have discussed this with confesses that it is difficult to quieten the mind. My experience is that as soon as I set
time aside for a quiet period in which I can listen to God,
distractions start pestering me like midges on a summer evening
in Scotland. As soon as I relax, the issues most pressing at the
time will come crowding in. I haven't mowed the lawns, I'm
behind with my writing, the bathroom needs redecorating, I've
forgotten to speak to so-and-so about an important issue raised
several months ago, and so it goes on. All of these matters
besiege my mind with a compelling urgency they did not previously have. Immediately I am distracted. I begin to feel restless. One part of my mind is trying to hold on to the problem,
the other part is trying to insist that I drop it so that I can go
back to silence. It becomes very difficult if new ideas for writing, or for sermons, pop into my head and I'm afraid I'll
forget them, or if possible solutions to existing problems occur,
needing immediate attention. Pushing these thoughts away
doesn't work, because, like a friendly indisciplined dog, the
more you push them away, the more they insist on having your
attention.

Some people find that the best way to deal with such distractions is to acknowledge them. This can be done simply by
making notes of the thoughts and ideas that seem important.
By doing this they lose their power to influence and distract
us. Many teachers on the spiritual life encourage the use of a
journal in which to record insights given during periods of
solitude. This helps to make our times of silence, even with
their distractions, a significant part of our spiritual pilgrimage.
Pushing thoughts out of our minds usually makes their intrusion
more effective. The reality of day to day pressure is best dealt
with when it is faced and included in the silence. Distractions
can then be transformed into milestones of progress rather than
rocks which cause us to stumble.

> Elected Silence, sing to me
> and beat upon my whorled ear,
> Pipe me to pastures still and be
> The music that I came to hear.[1]

Another positive aid in developing inner silence is to concentrate on our breathing. Hesychasm, from the Greek word for quiet, stillness, tranquillity, refers to the way of prayer practised in the Christian East from the fourth century. It encourages a form of prayer which is, as far as possible, free from words. It is a contemplative, thoughtful, reflective, non-conceptual form of prayer. In particular it commends a positive approach to our breathing as a means of direct communication with our inner life. In the *Philokalia*, a book of devotional instruction which comes from the thirteenth and fourteenth centuries, a master of the prayer life wrote,

> You know that our breathing is the inhaling and exhaling of air. The organ which serves for this is the lungs which lie round the heart, so that the air passing through them thereby envelops the heart. Thus breathing is a natural way to the heart. And so, having collected your mind within you, lead it into the channel of breathing through which air reaches the heart and, together with this inhaled air, force your mind to descend into the heart and remain there. Accustom it, brother, not to come out of the heart too soon, for at first it feels very lonely in that inner seclusion and imprisonment.[2]

St Ignatius spoke of rhythmical breathing while saying the Lord's Prayer, and obviously considered it a valuable aid to prayer. The rationale behind this is deceptively simple. No other physical function is as sensitive to our inner state than our breathing. States of anxiety, depression or fear produce rapid, shallow breathing patterns. Conversely, moments of relaxation, peace and enjoyment are marked by slower, deeper breathing rhythms.

Breathing is one physical function that can be controlled with comparative ease. Controlling our breathing rhythm by breathing more deeply and slowing down our breathing rate, is, in effect, a form of communication with our inner selves. It is as though we say to the turmoil within, 'Why are you panicking? Slow down and listen'. The word used for 'Spirit' in both Old and New Testaments comes from 'breath' or 'wind'. In a context which is focused on God, it is as though we are inviting the Holy Spirit to come into us, breathing his life and peace into every part of our being.

Concentration on breathing quietens the mind, the body and the emotions, but it also helps to point us away from the outer world of hurry and noise, towards inner silence and peace. The subject of inner silence, and how to develop it, and my treatment of it is, necessarily, incomplete. There is a wealth of good material, both old and new, available for those who want to take it further.

Accepting Spiritual Poverty

The most memorable sermon the world has ever heard begins with these words: 'Blessed are the poor in spirit, for theirs is the kingdom of heaven' (Matthew 5:3).

This verse has new meaning when we consider the value of solitude. Solitude involves a form of voluntary poverty, because we have to set aside all the personal and emotional props we have been using, and leave behind all the distractions and involvements with which we have numbed our spirits. To stand alone, naked and vulnerable in the presence of God is a fearful and, to some extent, humiliating experience. But the armour that has defended us against him must be cast aside, and we must relinquish the accumulated anaesthetics by which we have avoided our inner pain. Our sins would make us want to cover up, and our emotional rawness would make us reluctant to give up our spiritual and emotional palliatives, but we must take the risk of becoming poor in spirit if we are truly to meet with God. To be alone with God is to accept a voluntary poverty, setting aside those things that have made life bearable, but at the same time have numbed our sensitivity to his voice.

Loneliness has driven many in pursuit of distraction, it has also placed burdens on family and friends that are ultimately destructive. Loneliness feeds on self, solitude feeds on God. We must cross the threshold from loneliness to solitude, recognizing it is unlikely that this can be done without pain.

Juan de Yepes y Alvarez, a sixteenth-century Spanish theologian and mystic, known as St John of the Cross, speaks of this experience in a most vivid way as 'the dark night of the soul'. This has become a watchword for those attempting the transformation of loneliness into solitude.

It is frequently the case that a person, responding to a fresh impulse of God's love, makes a new commitment. This commitment has all the hope of new life but may be marked by confusion and desolation rather than states of joy. We may, in other words, experience poverty rather than riches. Part of the reason for this is in the compelling honesty of God who insists that we face the emptiness within and seek to fill it with his love and acceptance.

Many of us have constructed a flimsy camouflage, hiding the aching chasms within. This makes life bearable if we don't look too closely at what lies underneath, but it means we live on the surface. There is no depth to us. St John of the Cross, in his book *The Living Flame of Love*, explains this inner emptiness by using the metaphor of caverns.

These caverns are the soul's faculties; memory, intellect and will. They are as deep as are the boundless goods of which they are capable, since anything less than the infinite fails to fill them. From what they suffer when they are empty, we can gain some knowledge of their enjoyment and delight when they are filled with God . . .[3]

These caverns, the constituent parts of our personalities, are bottomless pits. They are the hiding place of our insatiable desires and restlessness. They contain monsters which have, in human terms, an appetite that cannot be satisfied. Such hunger and thirst can only be assuaged by the 'Infinite'. To try and fill these caverns ourselves is like throwing stones one by one into the Grand Canyon in the vain hope that one day we will fill it up.

The starting-point for us is to admit our spiritual poverty. We cannot satisfy the hunger within unless we meet with God. God in Christ is the bread which satisfies. He alone is big enough to fill our inner caverns and drive out the insatiable monsters they contain. Herein lies the pain. We have become so used to a handed-down faith. We survive on other people's spiritual exploits, and we get excited about the adventures and legends of the spiritual giants of previous generations, but we have little firsthand experience of God. To be sure, we know he loves us, and we may have some evidence of his presence in our lives, but we are fairly shallow. We have adopted a Santa Claus spirituality, worshipping a God who responds to our consumerist demands, but we give him no opportunity radically to affect the course of our daily lives. A glimpse into our inner caverns frightens us because we are confronted with our spiritual poverty, and instinctively we know we must deal with God alone.

When we read the classic writers on this subject we are told that the journey inward leads eventually to serenity, but our experiences as we begin are anything but serene. To have the courage to face our inner emptiness is costly. Why? Because we will have to admit we have wasted time, putting off for years what should have been tackled much earlier. We will also have to admit the searing poverty of our spiritual lives and lay aside the tailored front we have presented to the world.

Most of us know deep down that our inner life cannot support the claims we make for ourselves. Our busyness, which often brings us acclaim from others, we know is flight. To come

alone, unsupported, into solitude is like emerging from anaes-
thetic. We begin to feel the pain that previously was numbed
or deflected. The size and darkness of our inner emptiness
appalls us and, without considerable courage, we will run jab-
bering incoherently for safety, snatching back our props and
distractions. Like all births, birth into new life, a movement
from the secure to the unknown, involves pain. There is only
one way to make progress and that is to go ahead, stepping
out in faith. There can be no going back.

The paradox is at last revealed. In the words of Jesus, to be
spiritually poor is to be truly blessed. In acknowledging our
poverty, laying aside the glittering counterfeits of our sham
existence, we can trustfully reach out for God. The insatiable
longings within at last meet with the infinite love and mercy of
God. The dark night becomes an appointment with God, it is
no longer seen as desolation, rather as a threshold to new
things.

Facing the Desert

When we think of imitating Christ we more readily think of his
public ministry. Models have been given to us which focus on
power, with an emphasis on healing and deliverance as acts of
power. This is obviously very important but it is not the whole
story. Jesus spent thirty years of his earthly life in comparative
obscurity in Nazareth, and, before beginning his short public
ministry, spent forty days in isolation in the wilderness. We
also know that frequently he returned to the wilderness,
especially at moments of decision or stress. When we read the
New Testament and become thrilled with the person of Jesus
it is natural to be captivated by the things he did. Restoring
people's lives, healing the sick, raising the dead, speaking with
profound wisdom and simplicity into people's lives. Because
we are surrounded by such great human need it is almost
inevitable that we concentrate on trying to do the things he

did, in order to alleviate that need. The overall effect of this is that some Christians have rushed too quickly to the front line. They have hurried through Nazareth (the place of preparation), missed out the wilderness (the place of depth), and have presented themselves as fully operational, but inadequately prepared.

Enthusiasm for the battle, rather than spiritual preparation, has been the order of the day. Of course, no one would deny the value of enthusiasm, but spiritual warfare requires wisdom also. An inevitable result of taking short cuts to action is that we are presenting a generation of Christians who lack the inner resources to sustain a lifelong ministry. Jacques Ellul in *False Presence of the Kingdom* writes perceptively,

> What I am saying is that we are sending into the world babes in arms, who are not yet ready for adult tasks, that there is a preparation, both spiritual and intellectual, ethical and sociological, meditative and active, which is in *no way* being given to the Church, nor to those in the Church whom we are urging to become involved in the world.[4]

God is in less of a hurry than we are. It was fourteen years from the time of St Paul's conversion to the beginning of his missionary journeys. Those hidden years were no more wasted for him than they were for Jesus. They were part of the essential preparation for the task in hand. Many of the great missionaries and bishops in the Church were monks who were called out of monasteries. In a relatively short period of time they accomplished extraordinary feats of missionary and apostolic activity, because they were ready. Time spent alone in preparation for their task was vital to them. They emerged, as Jesus emerged from the wilderness, with supernatural ability to target the human heart with the gospel. They had faced themselves and their God and were ready. In another of the Beatitudes Jesus said, 'Blessed are those who hunger and thirst for righteousness, for they will be filled' (Matthew 5:6). These words would be misplaced, inappropriate and could safely be written off as mere religious sentiment, unless we recognize that it is in the desert that hunger and thirst are sharpened to the degree that they must be satisfied. The desert is the long journey each person must make alone with God. Henri Nouwen writes, 'To live a spiritual life we must first find the courage to enter into the desert of our loneliness and to change it by gentle and persistent efforts into a garden of solitude.'[5]

The modern search for spiritual satisfaction is a consumerist one. We try this church or that convention, this speaker or that counsellor, this technique or that teaching. We go from one human source to another, commuting backwards and forwards from Nazareth to Jerusalem. The spiritual nature of our search disguises, in half-understood truths, the fact that we are afraid to meet with God alone. We rush from one source to another trying to catch hold of drops of water to quench our thirst. Our surface puddles evaporate as quickly as they are created and we remain unsatisfied. This is a far cry from the promise given by Jesus of a spring of water that would constantly well up with life-giving freshness. We must face the fact that the wilderness is necessary to create a deep thirst for God.

What is this desert, this wilderness? For many of us it will be made up by the circumstances of life, much of which may be uncongenial and which we seek to avoid. Obviously, no one would want to enter a desert unless it was the only route to our destination. The things that cause us desolation could well be our personal desert. Bereavement, loneliness, conflict, unforgiven sin, unemployment, poverty, depression, unhappy relationships, disappointment; all of these experiences have the marks of the desert about them. There are a multitude of human experiences which are part of everyone's life, which may in fact be the wilderness we face. The restlessness of unfulfilled longing constitutes a desert in which we must face up to ourselves and to God. It is a threshold to be crossed. The very things we fear, and seek to avoid, could be the means God is using to prepare and shape us for greater work.

There is, however, another dimension to the wilderness. We have spoken of passive elements which may constitute a personal wilderness, but there is also the wilderness of deliberate choice. We know that in order to grow into maturity we must develop a life-style in which we can meet alone with God. Most of us cannot choose to leave our families and responsibilities simply to live a life of solitude, but we can learn to create an inner space which is deserted by all but God. This is not so much a series of spiritual decisions but a philosophy of life. Carlo Carretto wrote,

> Make yourself a little 'poustinia' (desert) in your house, in your garden, in your attic. Do not dissociate the concept of desert from the places where men and women lead their lives. Try both in your thoughts and in your lives to put this glorious phrase into practice: 'the desert in the heart of the city.'[6]

We can take this further and suggest that even for the busiest people living in the noisiest environments, inner space can be made for God. Brother Lawrence writes, 'The time of business does not differ from the time of prayer; and in the noise and chatter of my kitchen while several persons are at the same time calling for different things, I possess God in as great a tranquillity, as if I were on my knees at the blessed sacrament.'[7]

Spiritual depth will not be achieved unless we are prepared to be alone with God, and for most of us that means learning to be alone with him in the midst of community, noise and activity. We must locate our own desert in the market place.

But who will be our wilderness models? Can we look to the existing leadership of the Church, or to the Charismatic leaders? Important and gifted as many of them will be, they may not be up to this task. We will have to turn to our spiritual traditions, and to the other spiritualities of the Church, perhaps especially the Eastern Church, as our teachers.

Windows Outward

None of this, of course, implies that we are to devalue friendship, human love, or responsibility for the world. Quite the reverse in fact. Solitude does not isolate us from other human beings but makes real fellowship possible, because from the depths created in solitude we have something of ourselves to give. The concerns and needs of others, instead of skimming off the surface of our lives, will be taken into a life of reflection. Response can then be given from the depths of our heart, rather than off the top of our heads. Further, we will no longer feel the need to answer the questions others ask of us, but will be able to listen to the longings of their hearts and help them listen to their own questioning.

Solitude gives us an opportunity to distance ourselves from others, in order more easily to appreciate the gift of friendship they offer. Friendship is one of the loveliest gifts we can have, but sometimes our closeness to others prevents us from truly knowing them. Kahlil Gibran wrote, 'When you part from your friend, you grieve not; for that which you love most in him may be clearer in his absence, as the mountain to the climber is clearer from the plain.'[8] Thomas Merton spent the last few years of his life living as a hermit, but his life of solitude and contemplation brought him immense love for others. 'It is in deep solitude that I find the gentleness with which I can truly love my brothers. The more solitary I am, the more affection I have for them. It is pure affection, and filled with reverence for the solitude of others.'[9]

Solitude does not separate us from people, but, on the contrary, makes deep communion possible. As we face ourselves in the presence of God, so we can enter more deeply into the wonder of the Word made flesh. In one sense this consecrates all human life and makes me open to all others. The more honest I am about my own inner emptiness and weakness, the more I become at one with others. Christ became a man among men and women. Their stupidities, their heartaches, their restless loneliness are his also, and because they are his, they are mine. Paradoxically, my solitude has the capacity to make friends out of strangers.

Solitude, therefore, is not a movement of withdrawal, but it is a movement of engagement. It provides a window, set at a vantage point, through which we can contemplate the world in which we live. Instead of being a victim of the changing moods and directions of the world, we will be better placed to reflect on its needs, and nurture the struggling life around us.

Solitude can never be a self-indulgent fantasy, insulating us from the real world, but will give us an arena in which our responses will be alerted, and targetted with greater precision under the guidance of the Holy Spirit. The events in our society will become part of our contemplation. In this way our solitude will force us to live in the world. This paradox, exemplified in the life of Jesus, demonstrates that solitude brings us into closer contact with the world and creates true compassion.

Our journey in God is signposted by the pain and dereliction of the world. Crossing the threshold from our own restless loneliness into solitude enables us to feel the pain of others. Our inner thirst, sharpened by our own deserts of solitude, is to be the means whereby other life is nurtured.

Defeating Giants

A little girl wanted to know whether all fairy stories began with the words 'Once upon a time . . .' 'No', said her mother. 'Some begin, once I became a Christian all my problems disappeared.'

It is easy to give the impression that a relationship with God confers immunity from the stresses which affect the lives of every other citizen. Christians can imply that they possess some form of magic which prevents them from feeling grumpy in a morning or falling out with their spouses, or which makes their children behave impeccably. Such a Christian is presumed not to have problems with sexual temptation, always finds a parking spot, never stands in dog dirt and never misunderstands what people are saying to him. This Christian does not exist.

The fact is, we live in the same world as everyone else. We are subject to illness, accident and stress, just like everyone else. We do the same jobs, struggle with the same mortgage rates, watch the same TV programmes and eat the same food. We are heading for a different destination, but our route encounters the same pitfalls as all other travellers. We have the same trials and the same handicaps, our fears and failures are identical to all others.

One of my favourite books, given to me by a friend some years ago, is called *The Book of Heroic Failures*.[1] Reading it gives me a healthier perspective on life and enables me to see my failures with some degree of humour. One section, particularly appealing, is written on the subject of being wrong. It contains comments on people by so-called experts. 'We don't like their sound. Groups of guitars are on the way out.' So said the Decca Recording Company when turning down the Beatles in 1962. The group was also turned down by Pye, Columbia and H.M.V. 'Far too noisy, my dear Mozart, far too many notes.' So said the Emperor Ferdinand after the first performance of *The Marriage of Figaro*. The classic example is the comment of the Munich schoolmaster to the ten-year-old Albert Einstein, 'You will never amount to very much.' We can all be wrong about things, sometimes horribly wrong and, the fact is, Christians don't have a better track record than others. We may present ourselves as failure-free, but we are not.

One of my hobbies is to enjoy and maintain a 1937 Morris 10. One winter I put some time aside to do some restoration work on the car. To do the work properly I had to unbolt the front wings and remove the radiator surround and bonnet. Without these body parts the car looked a sorry sight; all the engine and vital components were exposed. It looked small and unhappy. There were struts and wires, cables and tubes, some covered in oil, others caked in mud. The smart, painted and shining exterior body panels disguised a reality that was somewhat different. It seems to me that many Christians are like this. They put a brave and shining face on things, but inside they feel pathetic and small and vulnerable. Somewhere along the line they have been exposed to the kind of teaching that assumes Christians don't make mistakes, don't have problems and don't experience failure or fear.

The subject of this chapter is fear. The giant that makes us look small. Christians who experience fear often hide it, because to admit to its presence implies that something is wrong in their relationship with God. Everyone experiences fear in one form or another; my plea is that we recognize it and face it. Experiencing fear is not a sign that we have failed as Christians, it is a sign that we are human. Pretending it does not exist, or burying it because it is too humiliating to admit to it are courses of action calculated to give the wretched fear a greater grip on our lives. Fear is one of the giants that, in one form or another, we all have to face and fight. It is a curious paradox that it is usually fear of very ordinary things, which to other people might seem ridiculous, that assume the proportions of a threatening giant in our lives. This chapter offers practical strategies for handling such fear on a day to day basis.

A Common Experience

Anxiety, worry and fear are very common emotions. Everyone knows what it is like to experience these things. I do not have to describe them to the reader. I have heard it said that the words most often repeated in the Bible are, 'do not be afraid'. In one sense this is quite encouraging because it helps us to understand that when we experience fear we are not abnormal. Quite the reverse in fact; we would be abnormal if we did not experience fear. Some fears are part of the human instinct for self-preservation and are necessary for our continuing safety. Fear of fire, or of driving on a crowded motorway in freezing fog would be examples of this. Such fear is healthy; encouraging us to treat these areas of potential danger with respect. It often seems that the situations people become phobic about are to do with areas of life that should be treated with care by everyone. However, in some people, the anxiety has become so extreme that it leads them to avoid all contact with the phobic situation. Fear of open spaces as being places of danger is a primal instinct bred into us by our ancestors. That is where the enemy would attack and destroy. This vestigial instinct can become the breeding ground for phobias in people today in situations where little or no danger is threatening.

Other fears are to do with the very substance of life; fear of illness, old age, unemployment and retirement. These fears exist because we live in an uncertain world and our experiences teach us that when such things occur the consequences are unpleasant. We all know people who have become ill, or old, or unemployed and their responses have served to confirm our view that such conditions are negative and therefore to be feared. We become fretful and anxious lest the same fate befall us. The condition that none of us can ultimately avoid, that of ageing, we seek to disguise by acting a part or pretending to be younger than we are. Older people who dress in clothing styles worn by their teenage children are usually displaying some element of this fear. Similarly, anxieties about finance and the practicalities of daily living consume large amounts of emotional energy, as does worry about a faltering marriage, or fears for our children.

There are fears that operate in the spiritual realm. Depressed Christians may ask, 'Does God really love me?' 'What if he rejects me?' 'My sin is too great to be forgiven.' We simply need to read the psalms to recognize that doubts about our spiritual condition can cause painful episodes of fear. Time after time the Psalmist feared that God would cast him off because of his sin. Time after time he was reassured that this would never happen. Nevertheless, such fears exist and severely depressed people can always find those verses in the Bible that suggest there is no hope for them.

Many fears are irrational. Some of the most extreme forms of anxiety and fear lead to phobic conditions which radically affect quality of life. Such fears stem from the complexity of our human personalities and the effects of early childhood experiences. Others are to do with the effects that severe emotional trauma and stress can have upon us.

As a pastor I meet people suffering from extreme forms of fear and occasionally discern that the cause is demonic. The appropriate ministry given to the local church to deal with this is the ministry of deliverance. This is to be undertaken carefully and prayerfully within the context of the local church. It must be pointed out, however, that this painful area of human experience attracts a lot of attention from those who believe all fear is demonic. A practical safeguard when trying to reach a decision about the need for deliverance ministry is to proceed only when the conclusion is endorsed by other mature and experienced Christian leaders. Most fear, although it may have a common root in the general purpose of Satan to harass and dismay God's people, is part and parcel of the condition of being human.

It would be good to think we can live without fear and anxiety, but most of us, for some period of our lives, will be unable to do so. It perhaps also needs to be said, as part of this discussion, that fear is not totally negative. We have noted the part it plays in keeping us alert to obvious danger; we also need to recognize that fear in mild doses can increase performance. Actors, musicians, sportsmen and women and public speakers often report experiencing fear as a prelude to their engagement, but acknowledge also that it can help to improve the quality of their performance.

In a study of American soldiers it was found that inexperienced troops displayed little fear and were careless about safety measures. More experienced soldiers felt fear, were more careful and, consequently, made fewer dangerous errors. Paradoxically, fear can help people deal with stressful situations. Dr Marks discovered in a study of people undergoing major surgery that patients who appeared fearless before surgery suffered excessive post-operative discomfort and showed more anger and resentment than did patients who had been moderately fearful before the operation.[2] By contrast, patients who had been highly anxious before surgery showed a lot of fear afterwards and complained of much pain and discomfort. Moderate amounts of fear can be beneficial; extreme fears are destructive.

God and Fear

Buried deep within many of us the thought persists that God is only interested in people who have sorted themselves out. To experience fear is taken as a sign of spiritual inadequacy

which will render us of little interest to God. It is heartbreaking
to observe this in people's lives and to realize that they often
feel so guilty about their fears that the last thing they want to
do is bring them to God. The presence of fear is seen as an
indicator that we have failed and therefore disqualifies us as a
worthy recipient of God's love. The assumption is made that
God will desert us to go and attend to a more worthwhile or
exciting Christian. The biggest mistake we can possibly make
is to assume that God's interest in us rises and falls according
to our spiritual state. Quite commonly, people will feel that
because there are so many world crises occurring, so many
more important matters and people to attend to, God couldn't
possibly be interested in the daily running of their lives. It
would be like asking Pavarotti to sing a jingle in an advert for
toothpaste, or a brain surgeon to attend to a grazed knee.

The remarkable thing about God, however, is that he *is*
interested. The God who created the heavens and the earth,
who brought life into being, who sustains the planets on their
allotted course, is concerned about the details of our lives. The
One who strides the heavens knows when our foot stumbles.
The One who nurtures all life provides our daily bread. The
One whose will is done in heaven has promised to protect us
from evil on earth. Such concern of the Infinite for the finite
is one of the most amazing facets of God's love for us. When
we look at the Bible we hear God saying to his people, 'Don't
be afraid, I am with you.' He is concerned when we are afraid
and wants to act to strengthen us against our fears.

To help us understand this more fully I want to consider the
story of the prophet Elijah; in particular an episode in which
we find him suicidal and depressed because of overwhelming
fear. One verse sums it up, 'Elijah was afraid and ran for his
life' (1 Kings 19:3). Here we see this extraordinary man of God
experiencing the characteristic symptoms of panic and terror.
It all began when Ahab became king of Israel. He was a
particularly nasty piece of work, with a wife called Jezebel,
who, if anything, was worse. She was forceful, domineering,

spiteful and determined to murder Elijah. Jezebel pioneered the worship of Baal, a Canaanite fertility god, and was fanatical in winning adherents. Inevitably, this brought her into conflict with the prophets of Yahweh and, in particular, with Elijah.

The central point of the story is the contest on Mount Carmel between Yahweh and Baal. Elijah, single-handed, challenged the 450 prophets of Baal, plus the 400 prophets of Asherah, to a death or glory test of authenticity. Two altars were built on Mount Carmel, two bulls prepared for sacrifices. The prophets of Baal were to call on their god, and Elijah on Yahweh. 'The god who answers by fire – he is God' (1 Kings 18:24). The prophets of Baal prepared their bull and called on the name of Baal from morning to evening. Nothing happened. Elijah taunted them. 'Shout louder,' he said. 'Perhaps your god is having a nap, or is busy doing something else, or has gone on holiday.' The prophets of Baal shouted louder and slashed themselves, dancing furiously and frantically prophesying until evening. But still nothing happened. Then Elijah said to the people, 'Come here to me.' Then he repaired the broken-down altar of the Lord. He took twelve stones, one for each of the twelve tribes of Israel, and rebuilt the altar in the name of the Lord. He dug a trench round the altar and commanded that the altar be soaked in water. Three times this was done, until water ran round the altar and filled the trench.

At the time of sacrifice, the prophet Elijah stepped forward and prayed: 'O Lord, God of Abraham, Isaac and Israel, let it be known today that you are God in Israel and that I am your servant and have done all these things at your command. Answer me, O Lord, answer me, so these people will know that you, O Lord, are God, and that you are turning their hearts back again.' Then the fire of the Lord fell and burned up the sacrifice, the wood, the stones and the soil, and also licked up the water in the trench. (1 Kings 18:36–8)

The amazed crowds were convinced, proclaimed Yahweh the

true God, and Elijah ordered the execution of the false prophets.

When Jezebel heard of this she was furious and immediately issued a threat on the life of Elijah. It is here we see him running away in terror, frightened for his life, praying that he might die. The power of God forgotten. So we see Elijah, gripped by fear, depressed, suicidal and on the verge of breakdown, steeped in despair. Recognizing that there may have been a predisposition to depression, it was clear that a number of other factors had made things more difficult for him. He was alone, or felt very much alone, both on Mount Horeb and now in the desert. He was physically tired, not only because of the stress of the conflict, but because he had also done a lot of travelling. He had run from Mount Carmel to Jezreel, a distance of approximately seventeen miles. Then he had fled from Jezreel to Beersheba, about a hundred miles, and was later to travel a further two hundred to three hundred miles from Beersheba to Horeb. There would also be quite severe emotional reactions after the trial by fire on Mount Carmel. This would have left Elijah low and vulnerable; the ideal conditions in which fear can gain ground and get out of perspective.

Fear, not God, was ruling the life of Elijah at this moment. But what is God's reaction? Does he reject the prophet? Not for a moment does he do this. The way God dealt with Elijah is very beautiful, moving and practical. He let Elijah sleep and then fed him. In other words, he looked after the prophet's most basic needs. He then brought Elijah to Mount Horeb so that he could speak to him and reaffirm his call. Horeb was the sacred mountain where God had made himself known. Elijah's return represents a coming back to the source of faith, to the very heart of God. In a most memorable way God listened to the complaints of the prophet and then spoke to him. He did not shout at Elijah in the strong wind, or knock his feet from under him by the earthquake, or burn him up in the fire, but spoke to him in the sound of a gentle whisper. Elijah was emotionally vulnerable, he needed God to speak quietly, reassuringly. Elijah was feeling small and fragile, so God spoke in a still small voice.

Because Elijah had been gripped with fear, he felt a failure, no longer fit to be used by God. However, God had other ideas. He gave the prophet something to do that affirmed his prophetic ministry. It was the responsibility of the prophet to anoint the king; very much as the Archbishop of Canterbury would crown the monarch today. Elijah was commissioned to anoint Hazael king over Aram, Jehu king over Israel and Elisha to succeed himself as prophet. Although this task was not completely fulfilled by Elijah, the meaning is clear. God still considered him valuable in the work to which he had been called. His fear had not rendered his ministry useless or invalid. Finally, God did something rather special for Elijah. Recognizing that one of his problems was loneliness, he provided a companion, a running mate in Elisha. Someone who would walk with him, sharing his burden.

Depression, anxiety, crippling fear can sometimes stalk the path of Christians. The last thing we must do is feel that we have failed. The story of Elijah shows how God responds when we are fearful and how watchful he is over the smallest detail in order to bring us into peace and wholeness.

Confront the Giant of Fear

Another Bible personality gives us a clue as to the best way of dealing with fear. Goliath had made the strongest warriors tremble with fear. It fell to the young, inexperienced David to face up to, and defeat this awesome giant. Fear has the ability to loom up in front of us as a huge frightening giant from which we want to run. All our instincts would put us to flight rather than encourage us to face up to our fears.

Of course, all of us have fears of one kind or another. For many people they take a mild form that can be relatively easily managed. The very common form of standing next to a cliff edge and feeling the compulsion to jump, can be dealt with by avoiding cliff edges, or simply fighting down the rising sensation of panic during exposure to the fears. Some, however, have fears which are much more powerful and have the potential to restrict life in a very distressing way. Thinking of Elijah again, his irrational fear of Jezebel restricted and isolated him to the degree that he reached the conclusion that death was the only way out.

This is a very sad fact. Sometimes, people who are facing extreme forms of fear would say that death would be preferable to the alternative of living in acute unhappiness. I want to focus for a while on those who, like Elijah, suffer this extreme form of fear. They are so gripped by it that the quality of life is radically affected. Many people suffer phobias and seek to manage their lives by avoiding the situations that trigger off the unpleasant sensations of terror. Some people have become so skilled at adjusting their lives around a phobia that family and friends are not really aware of what is going on. They may, occasionally, notice odd behaviour but nothing which pinpoints the seriousness of the situation. Admittedly, some acute fears are easier to hide than others. Fear of flying can be avoided by most people by them making it known that they prefer taking holidays in their own country. Agoraphobia or claustrophobia can be more difficult to conceal unless they are experienced in milder forms.

As I mentioned earlier, some forms have a spiritual origin which could point to the need for deliverance ministry. This is not a matter to be decided too quickly, but only after prayerful consideration by at least two mature Christians. Many local churches have people within the leadership who would deal with this. Most Anglican dioceses have advisors who could be consulted if there is uncertainty. If the conclusion is that deliverance ministry is necessary it should take place after proper preparation and with a minimum of fuss. If the person's condition does not radically improve after deliverance ministry, the cause is more likely to be psychological or emotional, and therefore needs to be handled differently. This is obviously where counselling and pastoral gifts are very important in the local church. My own experience confirms this. For years I had an irrational fear of flying. On two occasions I asked for prayer for this, both times from friends who are well-known Christian leaders and have been used in healing and deliverance. Their prayers did not set me free, but led me to the conclusion that the fear had to be tackled head on. This, I have discovered, is very important indeed when helping people with extreme forms of fear or who have phobias. God wants us to confront the fear strengthened by our relationship with him. I must face up to my own giants of fear and, though fearful, learn that I can trust God. Elijah discovered that he could face life again, and David could face up to Goliath, despite the immense fears that were gripping them. There is an extraordinary healing to be experienced as we face the giants of fear and discover to our huge delight that God will enable us to conquer them. It creates a sense of partnership, relationship and communion with God that is energizing, joyful and liberating. We are encouraged and become a means of encouragement to others. Fear can either make us despair or trust. When we take the risk of trusting God we find the door opens to new liberty and freedom. The first time I travelled by air I remember sitting next to a young boy who looked quite white, strained and obviously very nervous. I asked him if he was all right and, very bravely, he said he was. What he couldn't possibly have known was that I was also afraid. I had lost about a stone in weight because of anxiety about the flight. Incidentally, fear thrives through secrecy. The longer we are unable to admit to it, the worse it becomes, and the longer we refuse to confront it, the greater the hold on our lives.

Motivation

When facing up to fear, motivation is a very important factor. The Scriptures speak to us of a God who wants us to live free from fear. He did not create us to be bound by fears and live restricted unhappy lives. One of the marks of the presence of Christ the Messiah is that he sets the captive free. No one knows more about captivity than those who are afraid. Time after time the Scriptures affirm God's love and his purpose in setting his people free from oppression and fear. In a lovely verse in one of the psalms this relationship is clearly stated. 'I sought the Lord and he answered me; he delivered me from all my fears' (Psalm 34:4). Note the emphasis. The Psalmist asked God for help, which he was quick to give. He set him free from *all* his fears. God has made us to enjoy life and desires that we live without being restricted by fear. The beginning of our healing is to realize this truth and then to feel anger that the life God has given is being spoiled by fear. This is a good starting-point from which to set out to break the fear. Determination at this point is crucial. Fear will not be broken by half-hearted attempts to sweep it aside. We must get to the place where we are absolutely determined that God, not fear, should rule our lives. Life is too short. One day we will come to the end of life. Wouldn't it be awful if, at that moment, all we could feel was immense regret that we hadn't made the attempt earlier to break free from fear? People who have no fear may be fearless but they can never be courageous. Courage is that quality given to us by God that enables us to confront our worst fears, even though we may be quaking in our shoes. Be absolutely determined to live without being crippled by fear.

Preparation

As we determine to tackle our fears or face a phobic situation, preparation is important. Firstly, I believe we need to ask God to speak about our fears. If he wants us to be free he is going to encourage us. I have found that we can come to him in confidence and ask him to speak directly to our condition. He may draw our attention to a verse from Scripture, or plant in our minds an encouraging phrase. 'Don't be afraid, I am with you' might be an obvious way that he would speak. Sometimes a verse would stand out in a sermon, a daily reading, or come through a friend. I once remember turning the car radio on to just catch a verse from Scripture being used in the daily service. This was a great encouragement to me. If we truly want God to speak to us he will, and we will be surprised and delighted at how specific he is. Such verses should be recorded in a journal because they can be used for reflection and encouragement at a later date.

Secondly, we need to learn how to relax. Fear is made much more painful by anxiety and tension. Knowing about relaxation exercises and breathing rhythm can be enormously helpful, because through them we can learn to control physical responses to stress and quieten down our minds. Shallow, rapid breathing is associated with moments of stress and panic; deep breathing with peace and relaxation. Some techniques encourage a pattern of tensing and relaxing muscles throughout the whole body so that we can gain experience of controlling the body's reaction to stress. This is obviously invaluable. One might meditate on the Bible texts that have been given, or on a biblical scene. Sometimes I imagine a scene from the New Testament, using the details of the text to build the picture. Other times I might relive in detail a particularly pleasant experience, a walk by the canal, or in the Lakes, and simply picture Jesus walking with me, talking as we go. Not only is this a helpful form of meditation which builds up our relationship with Christ, but it is also a useful distraction technique. When our minds are under stress there needs to be some way of injecting a note of calm. It is very interesting to note that St Paul encourages an approach in which anxiety is replaced by prayer and reflection on good things.

> Do not be anxious about anything, but in everything, by
> prayer and petition, with thanksgiving, present your requests
> to God. And the peace of God, which transcends all under-
> standing, will guard your hearts and your minds in Christ
> Jesus. Finally, brothers, whatever is true, whatever is noble,
> whatever is right, whatever is pure, whatever is lovely, what-
> ever is admirable – if anything is excellent or praiseworthy
> – think about such things. (Philippians 4:6–8)

To be able to put this into practice by disciplining our minds
to concentrate on good things is a priceless gift well within the
reach of most people. Such discipline learned over a period of
time is a great asset when tackling a phobic situation or a major
area of fear.

Another way of fulfilling the same objective, that is, to get
our minds off our fears, is to pray for other people. To concentrate for a while on people whose needs are obviously greater
than ours. This can help us to get our own problems in perspective. We need to learn to speak and think differently, not
endlessly rehearsing our worries, but making the response of
faith. 'I can manage this with the help of the Lord, I know he
is with me.'

Another very practical tactic that can be helpful to employ
is to do with the transformation of symptoms. Specific physical
sensations often accompany extreme fear: dizziness, a pounding
heart, a sinking feeling in the pit of the stomach, palpitations,
profuse sweating, and the like. The very presence of these
symptoms can mark the onset of fear but they can also be given
another meaning. These, or very similar symptoms, also occur
when we are excited about something; meeting a special
person, going on holiday, receiving a prize, making a speech,
and the like. Instead of receiving them as the harbingers of
fear we can actually acknowledge them as sensations of
excitement at the prospect of confronting the fear and destroying its influence on our lives. David, faced with Goliath, must
have experienced similar sensations. We can receive them and

transform them, establishing them in our memory as the prelude to victory rather than defeat.

We also need to train our minds to take a long view. Fear confronts us in the immediate present; we may be going through a rough patch, *but we are going through*. We will emerge from the other end, in time we will be all right. We could picture ourselves looking back from a place of calm on the fear that has momentarily disturbed us. Next week, next month, we will see it differently.

I believe it is important to train ourselves in meditation, transformation and perspective techniques. They are a practical way of allowing the Holy Spirit to transform our minds into greater degrees of wholeness, and they prevent the mind from creating pegs on which unpleasant memories can permanently hang.

Act with Courage

Many people continue to suffer phobias and extreme fears because they feel they are powerless to do anything. They become passive and, as a result, more and more locked into their fears. It may come as a surprise to know that we can attack and destroy the thing which has had such a threatening and destructive influence on our lives. The best and most experienced warriors of Israel were dismayed and terrified by the awesome strength of Goliath; none of them dared face him. It was the young, inexperienced, unskilled David who alone accepted the challenge. Conventional wisdom may have judged him to be foolish in not realizing the dangers involved and in not using the best human means to protect himself, but he went ahead, using his own crude weapon, and protected only by his faith in God. The story, written in 1 Samuel 17, makes fascinating reading. To begin with, everyone, including Goliath, assumed it would be no contest. David, it was thought, didn't have a chance. David's own response, however, is very instructive. As a shepherd in the wild he had encountered marauding wild animals. A lion and a bear are specifically mentioned in the text, both of which he despatched with comparative ease. David is angry and scathing about the uncircumcised Philistine, Goliath, who had for too long had his own way: 'The Lord who delivered me from the paw of the lion and the paw of the bear will deliver me from the hand of this Philistine' (1 Samuel 17:37).

Fear can have an effect upon us far beyond its power to harm us. It looks like an immovable giant by which we feel cowed into surrender. Many submit unnecessarily to its threats who need not. We can be given courage to take on what appears to be impossible odds, recognizing that we are God's responsibility. At the very moment of confrontation, David had to know that God would keep his promise. If he failed to do this, David had no future. He would be painfully destroyed by a cruel brute of a man. The slender gossamer thread of faith which holds the balance between life and death, between peace and insanity, may appear pathetically fragile, but we have to know it is unbreakable. The weight of the whole universe, of heaven and earth, of all human life from the beginning to the end, of all the breath-taking reality of eternity, of all the hopes, longings and aspirations of every human being, can safely hang on that thread. David trusted God. His life never looked more tragically vulnerable or precarious than at that moment. But it was never more secure.

God has spoken to us about our fears. As we prepare to confront them we must reckon ourselves to be his responsibility. The bottom line cannot be read until we are in a position when everything depends on an act of faith. It becomes faith when there is no safety net. When God has spoken, we are as safe as it is possible to be. There have been many occasions when I have found myself thinking, as David must have thought, 'Lord, if you do not keep your word, I have no future.' Faith operates when there is no one but God to rely on. There is, in fact, great peace in reaching this point.

Another fact we need to know is a very practical one. Anxiety may be unpleasant but it is not generally harmful. The quality of life may be affected but people do not die from anxiety. However, a word of caution needs to be sounded. If someone with a heart condition or other physical disease has a phobia they want to confront, it is wise to consult the family doctor. He will advise about how much anxiety it is safe to experience at any one time. In this case, one would need to proceed more slowly, but progress can still be made. The doctor will also advise about whether further skilled help is required to assist in pacing the exposure to fear to the amount of anxiety tolerable. One of the most helpful books I have read on this subject is, in fact, written by a doctor, *Living with Fear* by Dr Isaac Marks. His very practical approach to the management of fear and anxiety is encouraging, not least because he raises the level of hope in the sufferer. The thing about fear is that it must be confronted. It thrives in secret and grows disproportionately when we run from it. Like David, we must determinedly place ourselves in the position where escape is not an option. The sooner our fears are faced the more rapidly they will fade. The longer the exposure, the less power fear will have over us. It will be clear that we are working towards increasing our tolerance of being in the feared or phobic situation. This must be done relentlessly until the situation we feared has become boring. If this can't be done in reality, do it by imagination. Envisage the worst and the present will feel better. It is, in fact, rarely the present moment that is unendurable. Fear of what might happen next is the thing that paralyses us.

It is only natural that we feel anxious and fearful during the process of confronting fear, but remember, courage is not the absence of fear, but a characteristic of those who face things *especially* when they are afraid. Don't run away from fear, carry on normal activities even while experiencing it. Wait for the intense flashes of panic to die down, perhaps employing one or more of the distraction techniques mentioned earlier.

The essence of dealing with fear is to learn to ride it until the storm passes. Having lived through it once we will be encouraged to face it again. Incidentally, don't be put off by any strange new nervous sensations that may occur as the fear is confronted. Satan, who uses fear as a tool, will try desperately to hang on to this part of our lives, even to the extent of bluffing us with new anxieties. The words of Jesus, 'Get thee behind me, Satan', are still the most effective. Exposure to stress helps us to build up a resistance to it and gives us confidence to go on, knowing that we can manage even when we feel overwhelmed. Remember, above all, that God is on our side.

From Fear to Faith

This is another important threshold, a doorway to pass through from a life that is ruled by fear to a life that is lived by faith. The Bible's invitation to live by faith means simply that we continue on our forward path no matter what is hurled against us. The dogs of fear may snarl and snap at our heels but they are chained. They cannot destroy us unless we allow it. This may be a startling truth for some to take hold of but, ultimately, we do have a choice. Either to live restricted and cowed by fear, or to live by faith. By that I mean having the courage to go on, even when fearful. The Bible emphasizes the potential of a mind renewed according to the Word of God. Everyday decisions will have to be made reaffirming our choice to live by faith, because every day new things to fear will rise up in our path to make us stumble. The moment comes for all of us when we must decide whether God can be trusted, and as we step forward, however tentatively, we discover the ground in front of us is firm ground. St Luke writes about the certainty of the Word of God (Luke 1:4). The word 'certainty' is translated from the Greek word *asphaleian* from which our English word asphalt derives. It is a non-slip, non-trip surface. To trust in God's Word means that we can walk ahead in faith, facing the most gigantic fears because he will not allow us to trip up. Dietrich Bonhoeffer writes, 'It is not our judgment of the situation which can show us what is wise, but only the truth of the Word of God. Here alone lies the promise of God's faithfulness and help. It will always be true that the wisest course for the disciple is always to abide solely by the Word of God in all simplicity.'[3]

One of my favourite psalms is Psalm 121, I read it especially when I am fearful.

> I lift up my eyes to the hills –
>   where does my help come from?
> My help comes from the Lord,
>   the Maker of heaven and earth.
> He will not let your foot slip –
>   he who watches over you will not slumber;
> indeed, he who watches over Israel
>   will neither slumber nor sleep.
> The Lord watches over you –
>   the Lord is your shade at your right hand;
> the sun will not harm you by day,
>   nor the moon by night.
> The Lord will keep you from all harm –
>   he will watch over your life;
> the Lord will watch over your coming and going
>   both now and for evermore.
>
>   (Psalm 121)

Living close to the Lake District I appreciate the opening sentence of the psalm. Nothing could be more beautiful or breathtaking than a view of the hills on a clear day; or more invigorating than to breathe the clean air; or more inspiring than to see snow on the ridges and hilltops; or more satisfying than to drink the rich cocktail of form and colour offered by the mountain slopes. The hills and mountains speak of strength and stability, of beauty and of peace. It is a powerful, vivid imagery, which may remind one of God, but is not, in itself, God. As the Psalmist wrote, it was likely that he had other things on his mind. Palestine was overrun with popular forms of pagan worship. Perhaps because of their beauty and grandeur the hills were used as sites for shrines and groves dedicated to pagan deities, to the sun, the moon and to nature. Here travellers could ask for a spell, a charm, an amulet or an enchantment to protect them from the perils of the road. They could ask the sun-god for protection against heat, or the moon-god for aid at night.

'Where does my help come from?' This is a pointed rhetorical question. Is it to come from the sun priest or the moon goddess, from Asherah or Baal? Remember, Elijah taunted the priests of Baal about their god's impotence and inactivity. 'Perhaps he is deep in thought, or busy, or travelling. Maybe he is sleeping and must be awakened' (1 Kings 18:27). People put their faith in the false promises of these false gods. If someone feared being tripped up by a demon as they travelled, they would buy the magic formula that would keep the demons of the road at bay.

'Where does my help come from?' Not from the hills. Beautiful and majestic they may be, but they are merely hills. The Psalmist's response to this question is clear and authoritative. 'My help comes from the Lord, the Maker of heaven and earth.' He looks, not to the hills, but to the One who made the hills. Psalm 121 rejects a religion of nature and creation, looking instead to the living Creator. He will not send you on your way clutching a magic charm, or mumbling an incantation against the demons of the road; he will walk with you and keep you from all evil. The priests of Baal were employed to wake up their god when someone needed attention; the Creator of heaven and earth needs no such prompting, 'he who watches over you will not slumber . . .' He will watch over our lives, our going out and our coming in. He will be there at our beginning and at our ending. He is the alpha and omega, nothing he promises at the beginning will ever fail even to the end. He is with us as we set out, as we travel, and he is still with us when we arrive. Fear need never dismay us. 'For you did not receive a spirit that makes you a slave again to fear, but you received the Spirit of sonship' (Romans 8:15).

The Cross spans the gulf between what we are and what we can become. It is the ever open door, inviting us into wholeness, it is the everlasting threshold across which we may step into that perfect love which casts out fear. With some foreknowledge of the Cross the Psalmist speaks. He is obviously not saying that we will never have pain or injury or distress; he is saying that no evil can possibly thwart God's purpose for us. No evil from any source can have ultimate power over us. Five times the Psalmist says that God will watch over us. In infancy, childhood, adulthood, middle age and old age; through all these seasons of life his love and protection will never fail. The door from fear to faith is flung wide open, we must step across the threshold.

8

Sexuality and Spirituality

Christianity is a very sexy business. This rather startling and, for some people, shocking comment came out of a conversation I had when I was doing some research for this chapter. In a modern and perhaps crude way, this tabloid expression had the effect of alerting me to a fundamental ambiguity. On the one hand, Christianity is a religion of the flesh (the Word became flesh), yet, on the other hand, Christians have generally found it hard to face the physical and sexual realities of faith. Frequently a double standard operates whereby we acknowledge the potency of our own sexuality and smoothly excuse our failures, while, at the same time, expressing Pharisaical horror when sexual scandal, particularly in relation to prominent Christian leaders, hits the headlines. Those who dare face up to their own feelings acknowledge the strong forces at work within their own sexuality and recognize that often they also are pushed to the edge. When reading of the apparent moral collapse of 'someone who should know better', the more honest amongst us will respond with quiet reflection, 'there but for the grace of God go I'.

This chapter is written with these paradoxes and perplexities as a background. It has the ordinary person in mind and does not claim to be a definitive treatment of the complicated interaction of gender and sexuality, nor does it deal with the sensitive area of human sexual problems. Its style is fluid, moving freely from general issues of sexuality to the more specific matters of gender and sexual activity, without definition or introduction. It is written in the hope that those who have struggled to understand their relationship with God in the light of their sexuality might have a new starting-point. But it is only a starting-point, as if putting a foot cautiously across a threshold to explore new possibilities. As a priest I have shared in the lives of many who labour under a heavy load of guilt heaped upon them by the Church. The 'thou shalt nots' have weighed heavily upon people struggling to relate the temptations and failures of life to a God who appears to demand perfection. They see, because this is how the Church has taught, that the commandments are prohibitions rather than means of grace. Many have not grasped the fact that the commandments do not so much accuse us of how evil we are, but remind us of how Christlike we can become. In other words, people need to be given new hope that God can *and will* forgive the sins and mistakes of the past and affirm his love for us as sexual beings. Moreover, we need to restore hope in God who freely gives grace to resolve the tensions and live with the ambiguities that arise simply from being human. I hope, therefore, that for many this chapter will mark a new beginning.

The problem really stems from the fact that God created us as sexual beings. The reality of falling in love, of sexual attraction, of having warm and close human relationships is very much what it's all about. To become a Christian does not insulate us from these factors; quite the reverse, it can heighten all of our senses and give us a far greater capacity for loving. It is not in the least bit surprising, therefore, that sexual temptation can be far greater after a person becomes a Christian. This may be a perverse logic to some minds, but we would be very foolish not to acknowledge it. In the light of this, my hunch is that God is far less surprised at failure in this respect than we are.

Sexuality and the power of sexual response is something that has always created fear and anxiety in religious people. Because of this fear, each religious tradition has worked out its own rules and restrictions to make life safe. A kind of damage limitation exercise. Unfortunately, though understandably,

Christianity has followed the same negative route, even suggesting, at particular periods of its history, that the pinnacle of
spiritual experience is to be attained by celibacy. In this way,
it has been supposed, the dangerous force of sex can be tamed
and rendered harmless. This, of course, does not work, as many
who have been called to celibacy will readily acknowledge. It
is like trying to tame a lion by putting it in a cage; it simply
increases frustration and stimulates a determination to break
free.

The spiritual impulse and the sexual impulse are probably the
two strongest in our lives, offering great potential for personal
fulfilment, but also opening us up to a great deal of pain. At
a fundamental level they have a lot in common. They both
offer immense pleasure and give rise to the richest forms of
creativity, but can also be used as tools to humiliate and
destroy. They both tap into the very springs of our personality
and exert a powerful influence on our development. We can
be moved to tears of joy or bitterness by our engagement with
these powerful mysteries. Both have extraordinary capacity
to raise us to the heights, or plunge us to the depths. They
undoubtedly have a common source and may well turn out to
be two sides of the same coin.

Part of the essential oneness between sexuality and spirituality is to do with their purpose. Both are to do with life-giving,
with creation, pro-creation and re-creation. Further than that,
they are both to do with expressing deep human need. Our
sexuality affirms our need for loving relationships with others,
and our spirituality evokes our need for God. But these things
are not separate. Our sexuality, at its best, works through
others to draw us to God, it is as though we meet in others the
incarnate Christ, God made flesh. In fact, we could go further
and say that sexuality, in affirming our need for 'an other',
creates in us a desire for 'The Other'. Sex never yields all it
seems to promise because the ultimate desire for union with
another human being can only be completely fulfilled by communion with God. Sexuality can never be reduced merely to

genital or sexual activity, it is to do with our creation as human beings made in the image of God.

The creativity and communion we seek through our sexuality trigger a hunger for the Creator himself. Many writers on Christian spirituality have sought to wrestle with this truth. Central to Karl Rahner's thinking, for instance, is the notion that at the core of every person's deepest experience, what haunts every human heart, is a God whose mystery, light and love have embraced the *total person*. God works in every person's life as the One to whom we say our inmost yes or no. We may deny this, ignore it, or repress it, but deep down we know that God is in love with us and we are all, at least secretly, in love with one another.

This is why living in Christian community is a risky business. Some people misinterpret the stirrings within them, understanding the inner deeper calling to a relationship with God only in human or sexual terms. So people launch themselves on a quest for love, falling in love with each other in order to satisfy the hunger within them. Striving to understand the mystery of sexuality is a primary function of spirituality. It is ultimately a search for integration, for wholeness. If only we could grasp the truth that our sexuality is a pathway to God. It is a rich human threshold, delighting us with its experiences of love, but beckoning us onward into a relationship with the Divine Lover.

A Path Uncertainly Travelled

If our sexuality is a threshold, a door opening on the love of God, it is a threshold across which many people step with great hesitation. It isn't difficult to understand this because no part of life is so surrounded with warnings, taboos and fears. To begin with, many people are unhappy with their bodies and feel ashamed or embarrassed when attention is drawn to them. To consider our flesh as wholesome, natural and enjoyable is

a quantum leap lots of us cannot make under any circumstances. This is obviously made harder for us because at every
turn we are presented with visual images of beautiful young
bodies which are invidiously presented as the norm. Watching
television, or flicking through glossy magazines, we are confronted with virtually flawless human specimens which simply
make us want to hide our bodies from view. We are given an
illusion to believe in which saps our self-esteem and guarantees
a life-long discomfort with our physical appearance. This, I
have no doubt, partially accounts for the current emphasis on
body building and health fads. There seems to be an almost
obsessional preoccupation with slimming and health issues generally, as though any sign of ageing must be eliminated at all
costs.

This is brought home to me in a good-natured way on a
regular basis by my super-fit young son. He is a six foot four
inch rugby-playing, weight-training giant. Looking down on his
father, whose hairline is rapidly disappearing down the back of
his neck, I can see the smirk on his face which means, 'that
will never happen to me'. But happen it will. The day will also
come for him when he will think twice about bending down to
tie his shoe-lace.

Furthermore, many of us have inherited views about sex
which make it difficult to be comfortable and open about the
subject. Sex instruction at my school, an all-male establishment,
was obviously a task none of the staff really wanted. Whichever
one of them drew the short straw clearly tackled the subject
with great reluctance. Mind you, that may not seem all that
surprising when you think of the attitude of most of the boys.
Their sniggers, jokes and innuendoes would have demolished
the self-confidence of even the most robust of teachers. All of
this adds up to the fact that sexuality is a subject we do not
generally feel at ease about. To wade red-faced through a sex
education lesson at school is one thing, to acknowledge that
sexuality is a pathway to God is quite another.

The matter is further complicated by the fact that sexuality, like all other human qualities, has its dark, shadowy side. Child abusers, women molesters and others who use sex as an instrument of destruction and humiliation cause us to hang our heads in shame. The cruelty by which some are exploited and damaged means that it is difficult sometimes not to be overwhelmed and made fearful by the shadow. In addition, we are faced with the appalling reality of the HIV/Aids scourge. Many people's experience, therefore, is that sex can scorch or wither rather than enrich; it can bring tragedy rather than joy and it can desolate rather than console. The fact is that in one way or another we are all sexually handicapped. This area of our lives breeds guilt, shame and fear and, like a garden with weeds, can soon be taken over by these negative emotions. The marvellous reality is, of course, that our sexuality is infinitely redeemable. Jesus took on human flesh so that forgiveness, healing and grace might restore us to fellowship with God. The great wound of the Cross can heal the scars of our humanity.

Reasons for the Dilemma

A friend of mine, who had spent some time working in Central Africa, showed me some photographs of the road conditions he had to contend with in order to do his job. The roads, alternately swamped by rain and then dried out in the scorching sun, were deeply rutted, making travelling very difficult. I heard a story about a sign which appeared alongside such a road. It said, 'Choose your ruts carefully, you will be in them for the next forty miles.'

The idea that sexuality is a pathway to God presents many of us with a concept which is hard to understand. It is a road which is deeply rutted, with many of us locked into ruts from which it is extremely difficult to escape. The two ruts which claim most travellers determining which inflexible route is to be taken, are those of social constraint and religious pressure.

This is a rather clumsy way of expressing it, so I will try and explain.

To a greater or lesser extent, our views about sex are formed by the society in which we live. Each generation has its own way of assessing both historical and current trends in sexuality. These trends are interpreted to form a core of belief which is presented to individuals whose attitudes are consequently shaped and directed according to the wisdom and insights it contains. A rather trivial example of this is contained in the once popularly held view that masturbation made one blind. This view is obviously no longer held and would be considered by most as laughable. Just as each of us has been, to some extent, moulded by those who gave us our first sex instruction, so our understanding of sexuality is shaped by the society in which we live. For instance, there is nothing new about homosexuality, but the way homosexuals today understand, not only their sexuality but also its form of expression, is quite different from the way it was perceived fifty years ago. Changes of attitude in the way society thinks about homosexuality have allowed such variations to occur.

The most radical changes have taken place in society's understanding about the sexuality of women. In the Victorian period, a woman was considered too pure and fragile to indulge the sexual appetites enjoyed by men. Carnality in women, sexual hunger in any shape or form, was considered improper, even unnatural. The popular myth of Victorian womanhood created a delicate, sexually frigid, angelic being, who was not supposed to have any sexual feelings. Those who did experience sexual pleasure were made to feel shame, contributing hugely to the levels of guilt and neurotic disturbance many of them experienced. Undoubtedly, many Victorian ladies who took to their couches with the vapours were suffering from sexual frustration and repression. Today, women are told that it is all right to enjoy sex. In fact, pursuit of orgasm is almost considered compulsory. This changed attitude has radically affected the way women feel and behave sexually. Thus, changes in attitudes to sexuality keep pace with what society as a whole considers appropriate.

The Biblical Puzzle

Because we live in a country which has been significantly influenced by Christian teaching and values, the Church has had a major responsibility in shaping society's attitudes to sexuality. But here we have problems. The Church gives mixed messages as though it were uncertain about the subject itself, unable accurately to discern the contours of the gift as distinct from its shadow. Ambiguities abound, stemming from age-old conflicts within the Church, especially in understanding the relationship between flesh and spirit. The flesh is considered to be at war with the spirit and needs careful restriction and control if the spiritual life is to survive intact. Nevertheless, the lurking suspicion that God created our bodies to enjoy our sexuality will not altogether go away. This ambiguity is partly to do with the different approaches to the subject that one might perceive in some of the writings of Scripture. For instance, consider this passage:

> Let him kiss me with the kisses of his mouth –
>   for your love is more delightful than wine.
> Pleasing is the fragrance of your perfumes;
>   your name is like perfume poured out.

This, as many will recognize, is the opening verse of the Song of Solomon. The rich language used here, and also later on in this extraordinary book, is unashamedly borrowed from the intimacy of sexual love. Compare it with some of the rather impatient, unromantic statements of St Paul: 'It is good for a man not to marry. But since there is so much immorality, each man should have his own wife, and each woman her own

husband . . . for it is better to marry than to burn with passion'
(1 Corinthians 7:1, 2, 9).

I know that these are different kinds of literature and were
written for different reasons. Nevertheless, it is not too difficult
to see that lying behind them are two different attitudes to
sexuality. The tenderness and excitement of human sexual love
portrayed in the Song of Songs are clearly absent in the Corinthian verses. St Paul appears to want to deal with the incon-
venient practicalities of sex in order to concentrate on more
important matters. He is, however, honest enough to acknowledge that some of his ideas do not have the authority of the
Lord behind them; they come from his own understanding.

It is not difficult to see, therefore, that at times when the
Church was facing periods of uncertainty in regard to sexual
morality, it would emphasize what were considered to be the
cautious and corrective views of St Paul, in order to ensure
that members of the Christian community did not step out of
line. Given the nature of life and the importance of sex, there
can't have been many periods in the Church's history when it
wasn't having to deal with the consequences of sexual excesses.
The second-century Gnostics, who had a very powerful but
discordant influence on the Church's understanding of sexuality, are a case in point. They mixed a confusing cocktail
of ideas about sex, matter, maleness and femaleness into an
unpalatable brew. Physical matter was an unfortunate accident
resulting from a tragic dislocation of the spiritual world.
Woman, the undisputed inferior, would find redemption by
absorption into her guiding principle, the male. He would bring
form and shape, direction and purpose, to her misshapen existence. The penis, a current euphemism for which was 'the
Necessity', would be the instrument of such a transformation.
This was fighting talk, even by second-century standards.
Sexual intercourse, which for some Gnostics was a dark and
shadowy activity to be overcome by the redeemed, became for
others a hobby, earning accusations of immorality for many

Gnostic teachers. This, as you can imagine, was a matter of no small importance for the leaders of the Church.

The fear this aroused in bishops and theologians led, quite understandably, to over-reaction, with emphasis placed on those parts of Scripture that would, it was hoped, redress the balance. Traditions have therefore developed within the Church which have a cautious and, subsequently, negative attitude to sex and sexuality. These traditions have predominated to the extent that a more positive approach has been overshadowed, if not completely lost, on the way.

The task of theologians throughout the ages has been to give a credible theological justification to this negative sexuality. Some of the most powerful theologians the Church has ever known set about this task, in successive generations, with incredible efficiency.

It was, however, an efficiency stalked by ambiguity and double-think. The Christian anxiety about the flesh and all the evils to which it is subject, co-exists uncomfortably with the doctrine of incarnation. On the one hand, the Church acknowledges the wisdom of God in sending his Son to be born of human flesh, while, on the other hand, condemning human flesh as sinful.

Sex – a Christian Neurosis?

Karen Armstrong lays the blame for this state of affairs on a kind of Christian neurosis which exists alongside official Christian teaching and, at the same time, contradicts it.[1] 'To embrace a woman', wrote Odo of Cluny in the twelfth century, 'is to embrace a sack of manure.' How could he write these words in the light of The Song of Songs which, among other things, celebrates the physical joy of womanhood? Furthermore, how could he and other Fathers of the Church speak in such a derogatory way about women, especially since Jesus was born of a woman?

So it has been throughout the ages, in repeated acts of double-mindedness, that the Church has sought to defend the biblical truth of the beauty of sexual love, while at the same time, creating an emotional climate which led Christians to conclude that sex was evil and abhorrent. St Ambrose is often mentioned for his emphasis on the holiness of marriage, but is also quoted as saying, 'virginity is the one thing that keeps us from the beasts.' St Augustine, St Thomas Aquinas, Luther, Calvin – all of them – displayed signs of this double-minded attitude to sexuality and left an unhappy legacy for future generations of the Church. It's as though they all struggled with the subject, and out of the struggle emerged an almost entirely negative attitude to sexuality within the official Church.

'How foul and horrible a thing sin is, for lust is the only thing that cannot be cured by any remedy! Not even by marriage, which was expressly ordained for this infirmity of our nature' (Luther's Commentary on Genesis 3:9).

The link between sin and sex is a deep one permeating every level of our thinking and creating immense problems of guilt for humankind. The Church has not been able to set people free to enjoy sexuality. It has tried to encourage a high view of sex on the one hand, while creating an emotional climate which was calculated to prevent people from enjoying it, on the other. An impossible and confusing stance, which has led the Church, at particular moments of its history, to attempt to regulate sex in such a way that it has had all the appearance of a comic farce.

Thus, in the Middle Ages, the Penitentials (a sin-scale, giving guidelines to the clergy to show them how to rate particular sins) forbade sex while a woman was pregnant, menstruating or breastfeeding. Given the lack of contraceptives and the consequent frequency of pregnancy, this radically reduced the opportunity for the average couple to indulge. As if this wasn't enough, sex was also forbidden during Lent and Advent, on Ember days and also on Sundays, Wednesdays and Fridays. It was discouraged before receiving communion and, in the later Middle Ages, on Thursdays, in honour of Jesus' arrest, on

Fridays because of his crucifixion, on Saturdays because it is Our Lady's day, on Sundays because of the Resurrection and on Mondays in commemoration of the dead. Frequent fasting was also recommended to the faithful. So, if a couple could find the odd half hour on a de-restricted Tuesday which was free from the Penitential prohibitions of pregnancy, menstruation and breastfeeding, sex was probably the last thing on their minds.

Holiness and Passion

There is a curious irony at the heart of this matter. Nothing is more revered by the Christian than Christ's Passion, and nothing more feared than human passion. Despite all that has been written and said in recent years that is positive about sexuality, one doesn't have to dig very deep to unearth the Christian unease about passion. Try as we may, Christians have great difficulty with the thought that passion, especially sexual passion, might have anything to do with the process of spiritual growth. The thought that sexuality may be as significant a factor as prayer in our spiritual development, is a concept too difficult to grasp.

For so long the Church has implicitly taught that sex, though it is necessary to produce children, nevertheless, has no creative holiness in its own right. Yet even here we are guilty of a sad duplicity. Many people, Christians included, have acknowledged the spiritual significance of passion in the world's great tradition of literature. Abelard and Heloise, Tristan and Iseult, Lancelot and Guinevere, Dante and Beatrice have stirred generations of readers with the spiritual and creative quality of their love, despite the fact that, from the point of view of Christian morality, it was illicit. How tragic that we can applaud passion and see its power for good in the legendary heroes of literature, but hardly dare to acknowledge its good purposes in our own lives.

However, holiness, if it has any meaning at all, must belong to this life, to the ordinary things of this world. One of the greatest Christian truths, the one that gives Christianity its uniqueness, is that God made his home in a human body. We are body as well as spirit. If Christ could be at home in a human body, ought not we to be at home in ours? Our sexuality is just as much a vehicle for the power and love of the Holy Spirit as is our spirituality. Of course, sexuality can be perverted and used destructively, but so can the spirit. Immeasurable suffering has been caused by people who act according to the dictates of their particular brand of spirituality and who consequently wreak havoc in the lives of those around them.

Spirituality is nothing other than the whole of life offered to God as a sacrifice of praise. Words like surrender, adoration, devotion and love are commonplace in the Christian's vocabulary when seeking to express a relationship with God. The connection we need to make is that these are also the words used to express human passion. It is as though, in our experiences of human passion, we are reaching out to the One who is the author of that passion. Our earthly love is a marker, a pointer towards heaven. Traditional Christianity has given us a mountain of literature written to persuade us to mortify, or subdue, our passions. Precious little is given to help us to see the truth that our sexuality is a pathway to holiness. This is despite the fact that the Scriptures give us the image of sexual love as being the unique and passionately expressive model for understanding the love of Christ for the Church. 'The saint may mortify his passions, but they remain a condition and even an element of his holiness. For holiness is itself a passion . . .'[2]

Mary Magdalene – a Person on the Threshold

I return to the familiar figure of Mary Magdalene as an illustration of my point. As indicated earlier in the book, I ask the reader to accept the tradition which identifies Mary Magdalene,

Mary the sister of Martha and Lazarus, and the woman mentioned by St Luke as the woman who had lived a sinful life, as one and the same. This woman presents us with an image, a picture of someone who unashamedly used her sexuality as a vehicle for worship. For her this was a moment of transformation, a movement across the threshold into forgiveness and new life.

Now one of the Pharisees invited Jesus to have dinner with him, so he went to the Pharisee's house and reclined at the table. When a woman who had lived a sinful life in that town learned that Jesus was eating at the Pharisee's house, she brought an alabaster jar of perfume, and as she stood behind him at his feet weeping, she began to wet his feet with her tears. Then she wiped them with her hair, kissed them and poured perfume on them. (Luke 7:36–8)

In a reckless, extravagant, disorderly gesture of love, Mary won the heart of Christ just as certainly as she roused the suspicion and anger of the bystanders. People are usually most critical of those who do things they do not understand, or which make them feel uncomfortable. This act clearly stirred up powerful emotions in those watching, to the extent that they had to try and discredit Mary. This they did in a pathetically crude and familiar way, by questioning her motives and by undermining her as a person. In Luke's version Jesus was reminded that this woman was a sinner, and in John's account the wastefulness of the action was emphasized. The reality is, however, that it was all a thinly disguised attempt to discredit her because her action had touched everyone at the deepest possible level. It made full and unashamed use of human, earthy passion in a gesture of adoration that challenged to the roots the religious and human experience of all who saw it happen.

Pascal has said, 'Passion cannot be beautiful without excess, one either loves too much or not enough.' Christianity has helped to create a fear of passion, a neurotic anxiety about excess which has led to the commendation of mediocrity as a desirable virtue. This view has little to do with Jesus of Nazareth who would regard with incredulity the flesh-hating teachers of the Church who have left us such a bloodless legacy.

Passion is to do with being in a human body. We speak of Christ's passion as being expressed in and through his human body; it has no meaning other than when it is clothed with human flesh. He therefore does not have the difficulty many of us experience, of understanding that passion is an important strand in holiness. We cannot be truly holy until we acknowledge the existence of passion and recognize it as a pathway towards a deeper relationship with God. Another point of contact between the Passion of Christ and human passion is to do with suffering. Christ's Passion led him inexorably to the Cross, true human passion will also take us the way of the Cross. Passion is a renunciation as well as a discovery, a sacrifice as well as a delight. It is a friend, not an enemy, to our desire for God. Whether out of desperation or not, we do not know, but we do know that somehow Mary crossed the threshold and found to her utter joy that Jesus accepted her sexuality as an offering of herself.

Far too many of us are locked into a conviction that passion, especially sexual passion, is questionable. We have an extraordinarily wide vocabulary that deals with the mortification and subjugation of passion, but so very little that speaks of it as a gift. Happily, Mary seemed to have none of our reservations, or, if she had, she had been set free from them. Her sinful use of her sexuality had been forgiven. As a consequence, she gave us one of the most beautiful passages of Scripture that shows that human sexuality and spiritual passion are like rivulets that can flow into each other, nurturing us into holiness.

Humility, the noblest of all virtues, derives from the word *humus*, meaning earth. That which is most earthy is also, potentially, that which is most holy. That is why Jesus could see so clearly the image of God in the earthy passion of Mary. He gave her permission to be herself, to offer her womanhood as an act of unashamed devotion. He was less concerned about her past, with all of its mistakes, than he was with what was happening to her now. What was once seen only in the context of lust is transformed by love into an act of worship totally acceptable to the Son of God. This should not surprise us at all because, according to his own understanding of his ministry, he had come to call such people into the Kingdom of God. He had not come, he said, for the righteous and pious, but for sinners – the traitors, the sexually promiscuous, the thieves – they fit into his scheme of things. The Kingdom of God is for such as these.

Celibacy

Something needs to be said at this stage about celibacy, or singleness. The Church has long had a noble tradition of men and women who feel called to remain unmarried and have therefore renounced sexual activity. At some point towards the end of the second century, Galen wrote about Christians: 'Their contempt for death is patent to us every day, and likewise their restraint from intercourse. For they include not only men but also women who refrain from intercourse all through their lives.'[3] In similar vein, Justin spoke proudly of those Christians who were able to exercise sexual restraint: 'Many, both men and women of the age of sixty or seventy years, who have been disciples of Christ from their youth continue in immaculate purity . . . It is our boast to be able to display such persons before the human race.'[4]

The sub-text of these writings contains just a hint of a problem that was later on to cause difficulty. By the end of the second century virgins, or celebates, established a distinct élite in the Church. These people remained virgins and created an aura in which sexual abstinence was seen to be a mark of outstanding spirituality. It was but a short step to seeing sex as a hindrance to spiritual growth.

Be that as it may, there are still many Christians who see celibacy as a significant part of their discipleship. There are also others who, for various reasons, are unlikely to get married. It is important to recognize, therefore, that for a person to forego sexual activity does not imply that they are denying their sexuality. Quite the reverse, it is especially important for the celibate to accept their sexuality. Many who have taken a vow of chastity talk, not of something they are giving up, but of a gift they are receiving. Virginity need not negate sexuality, rather it can enhance it and cause the human qualities of maleness and femaleness to be focused in a rich and attractive way.

Perhaps there are opportunities for the single to explore their sexual polarity to a greater degree; the male accepting and cultivating feminine aspects of their personality, and the female the masculine. This thought contains immense possibilities for wholeness. God created human beings in his own image, he also created them male and female. The separation of the male and female principles in each person is a symptom of disintegration, leading to unnecessary and unedifying gender conflict. Chauvinism, both male and female, is an uncomfortable fact of life, spoiling relationships and denying people the opportunity to be generous with one another. Movement towards unity of maleness and femaleness within the individual is a movement towards wholeness. Could it be part of the vocation of the celibate to offer us all, in this respect, a healthier example to follow?

Earlier Christian themes of renunciation and celibacy strike a discordant note in the modern ear, yet, as the life of Christ and other celibates demonstrate, the single life need lose none of the rich warm qualities of human sexuality. Some of the celibate priests and nuns that I have had the privilege to get to know over the last few years, remarkably demonstrate this truth.

Metanoia

Metanoia, meaning a change of heart, mind and direction, is one of the most exciting words in the New Testament. It is exciting because it holds before us the prospect of a life made completely new by the love of Christ. Metanoia is at the very heart of the gospel, inviting us into a relationship with Christ that sets us on the road to transformation and renewal. It is to do with returning to the source of all life, to have our eyes opened to see all things differently. Supremely, it is to do with a renunciation of our old, pre-Christian ideas of God. The first idea we must renounce is the idea that God is a God of vengeance, who apparently enjoys seeing us squirm under the impossible weight of our sexuality. We are welcomed into what Stephen Verney has called a 'dance of love' with God, herein to celebrate our creation as men and women on whom the love of God so gloriously and persistently rests. In Christ the divine and the human are in perfect harmony celebrating the marriage of heaven and earth. However faintly perceived, this is a mirror image of the relationship between sexuality and spirituality, it is earth and heaven bound together within the framework of the human personality.

Metanoia is the change from the grasping 'I' to a resting in the 'I AM'. It is a movement from the egocentric to the Christocentric, bringing light to the dark and confused thinking which has progressively reduced the richness of a total sexuality merely to forms and variations of genital activity. It is a threshold across which we step, separating the manipulative self from the surrendered self. Through metanoia we are born anew, carried joyfully into a new environment in which God listens to the deepest desires of our hearts. As Mary poured out her love for her Lord, so he received it with pleasure, thus affirming her as a person and giving her sexuality meaning as a form of holiness and grace. Her passion, previously abused by herself and others, is not stemmed by Christ but is transformed and channelled by his love.

It is a universal law that the pursuit of happiness results only in its loss. Mary Magdalene, along with countless others, made that painful discovery. But all is not lost, the change of direction made possible by the Cross, also makes available a completely new power of love. A word that goes well with metanoia is the Greek word 'agape'. This is the word for love used most often in the New Testament and which takes us beyond the realms of biological or emotional response. Its use signifies a radical change in the human personality, focusing far more upon the needs and well-being of others than on our own. It is the difference between a mirror and a window. A mirror enables us to see only ourselves, a window all others.

Meister Eckhart, a thirteenth-century German Dominican mystic, uses an evocative image, suggesting that instead of letting our passions run away with us, or penning them up so that they cannot break free and cause damage, we put on them the 'bridle of love'. In all of this Mary Magdalene gives us a reassuring and inspiring model to follow.

The Song of Ascents

A worrying and, to some extent, depressing factor of twentieth-century Christianity is the consumerist attitude many Christians seem to have to their faith. Church-hopping is a phenomenon clergy, in the latter stages of this century, are having to come to terms with. People are easily bored with what is happening in their own community, and are constantly on the look-out for new spiritual thrills. People become Christians, make a commitment to their church, but as soon as they hear of something more exciting elsewhere, go wandering off in search of a new experience. It is not unusual, therefore, to observe groups of excitable Christians, with the breaking strain of a Kit-Kat, cutting loose from their own church and taking to the road in order to taste the new religious flavour currently on offer. The quest may be for a new spiritual feeling or a visit to a sacred religious shrine, but the effect is just the same. Clergy and Christian leaders often find themselves forced into the role of tourist guide, giving people information about the beauty spots and high points of the faith instead of preparing them for a journey of faith.

We are not tourists but pilgrims. Without doubt we are on a journey, but the goal is maturity not entertainment, service not self-indulgence, worship not narcissism. Emphatically, the journey is to be undertaken with joy, but it is a joy fashioned in the valleys of experience as well as on the heights. Tucked away in the Hebrew Psalter is a distinct group of psalms (120–134) which are called the Songs of Ascents. They are generally understood to be the songs Hebrew pilgrims sang on their way to Jerusalem, the Holy City. But the ascent was not only the literal pilgrimage to Jerusalem, it became a metaphor, symbolizing the life of pilgrimage. St Paul described it in this way: 'Forgetting what is behind and straining towards what is ahead, I press on towards the goal to win the prize for which God has called me heavenwards in Christ Jesus' (Philippians 3:13–14).

The Christian life is a pilgrimage advancing from one level to another. It is a Song of Ascents as we grow into maturity from one degree of glory to another. Such a life requires of us a long vision and steady progress towards the goal. We are encouraged to use the heights to get our bearings, to refresh our vision and sense of direction, so that we can negotiate the valleys with some degree of accuracy.

This chapter is about the journey. I am basing it on a piece of spiritual literature that has meant a great deal to me in recent years. Its discovery was one of those rare moments, a brief flash of light, which simultaneously illuminated a number of dark corners in my understanding of the Christian way. It was for me, and I hope will become for others, a threshold across which we can step into greater enlightenment.

St Bernard of Clairvaux's spiritual masterpiece *On the Love of God* (*De Diligendo Deo*) contains his teaching on the Four Degrees of Love, the pathway to maturity. The first degree of love is the love of self for self's sake. The second degree is the love of God for self's sake. The third degree is the love of God for God's sake, and the fourth degree is the love of self for God's sake. It is like a song of ascents encouraging us forward and onward, inviting us to keep pace with the drumbeat of heaven.

A word about Bernard. In 1953 Pope Pious XII issued an encyclical celebrating Bernard as the Doctor Mellifluous, which means 'with words sweet as honey'. In his book *The Last of the Fathers*, Thomas Merton linked Bernard with Psalm 46:4 describing him as a stream of that river which makes glad the city of God. At the age of twenty-two Bernard entered the monastic community of Citeaux in Burgundy. He took with him a large contingent of family and friends; an uncle, four brothers and twenty-five of his friends. Later, he was sent with a band of other monks to found another monastery at Clairvaux. As Abbot of Clairvaux, Bernard became the most dynamic figure of the twelfth century, if not the Middle Ages, consulted by kings, popes and ordinary people alike. Clairvaux flourished, becoming famous for its wines and for the presence of Bernard himself. Dante thought so highly of Bernard that, in his pursuit of Beatrice into Paradise, he reached the tenth sphere of the heavenly mysteries, saying:

> I thought I should see Beatrice, and saw
> An old man, habited like the glorious people;
> O'erflowing was he, in his eyes and cheeks
> With joys benign, in attitude of piety,
> As to a tender father is becoming.[1]

This is the Bernard who through his writings, his sermons and his spiritual influence played a major part in the development of Western Christendom.

The Love of Self for Self's Sake

The starting-point for all of us is love of self for self's sake. Bernard assumes this to be natural and good unless it leads to rank self-centredness in which case it must be disciplined and corrected by love of God and others. This natural love of self can, like a very strong current, burst the banks of self-control, flooding the field of self-indulgence. A commandment, like a reinforced river bank, is then necessary. 'Love your neighbour as yourself' is the commandment Bernard commends as the appropriate corrective.

In the spirit of self-sacrifice which marked Bernard's life, and the lives of those he lived with in community, this may have been a relatively straightforward matter. However, many of us are coloured by a different stripe. We live in a world in which the worship of self has become a way of life, if not a religion in its own right. Bernard is accurate when he says the starting-point is love of self, but it may no longer be possible to assume that this self-love is even broadly capable of staying in line with reasonable natural expectations. The irony in the jibe about the self-made man who worships his maker, comes uncomfortably close to the truth.

The influence of secular humanism, through a plethora of selfist philosophies, has led to the creation of a very powerful doctrine of selfism which is diametrically opposed to Christian teaching. The biblical emphasis on denying the self is placed on the level of a quaint fable by modern enlightened minds. Self-fulfilment, self-actualization, discovering the self, quite reasonable aims in the right context, have become the central doctrines of a new religion. Selfism, according to Professor Paul Vitz, is the word that describes how secular humanism has been developed into a cult of self-worship.[2]

Professor Vitz, in his very useful book, *Psychology as Religion – The Cult of Self Worship*, offers an analysis of selfist ideas and compares them with Christian teaching. He points to the influence of Feuerbach, a nineteenth-century German philosopher and disciple of Hegel, who led a powerful attack on Christianity. Other thinkers, whose ideas about religion were influenced by Feuerbach, include Engels, Marx, Huxley, Nietzsche, John Stuart Mill and Freud. Feuerbach wrote a book called *The Essence of Christianity*, which argued against the divinity of Christ and the existence of God. His basic premise was that theology, the study of God, should be resolved into anthropology, the study of humankind. A sample quotation makes the point:

But that which in religion ranks first – namely, God – is, as I have shown, in truth and reality something second; for God is merely the projected essence of Man. What, therefore, ranks second in religion – namely, Man – that must be proclaimed the first and recognised as the first.

If the nature of Man is man's Highest Being, if to be human is his highest existence, then man's love for Man must in practice become the first and highest law. Homo homini Deus est – man's God is MAN. This is the highest law of ethics. THIS IS THE TURNING POINT OF WORLD HISTORY.[3]

The movement of society from a religious to a humanist base has been thorough, so much so, it is generally assumed that those who go on to higher education will, at some stage, have abandoned their faith.

The secular humanism of Feuerbach, which sought the transcendence of self in the love of humankind, takes a strongly anti-Christian stance, and has been popularized and made palatable, by many self-theorists. A welter of literature has been produced which makes selfism an acceptable, pseudo-Christian doctrine. Many of the self-help theorists with their language of self-actualization and self-realization fall into this category. Catch-phrases such as: 'be a friend to yourself', 'I'm OK, you're OK', 'create your own happiness' abound in selfist literature.

Soggy Christian minds have lazily taken on board a humanist notion of the self dressed up in superficial Christian language. Part of the problem is, of course, that there is a resonance between some of these thoughts and biblical teaching. Jesus bids us love our neighbour as ourselves. This obviously contains the notion of self-love, and may explain why many Christians are taken in.

It is important, however, to recognize, along with Bernard, that the love of self for self's sake, at its very best, can only be the starting-point. At its worst it gives rise to a sickly narcissism which is anything but Christlike. People in love only with themselves will have no competition and will live a desperately lonely life. The One who gave us freedom to love self as we would love our neighbour, also told us to *lose* self. Self-denial, not self-actualization, may yet turn out to be the most accurate and fulfilling route to true self-love.

The Love of God for Self's Sake

The second degree of love is the love of God for our own sake, or more particularly, the love of God for what he gives. People begin to love God, not for his sake, but for their own. This is a stage all of us go through, although some appear to become stuck at this point. Many Christians get no further than a 'blessing-centred' experience. They look to God for help when they are in trouble, but do not particularly seek to stay close to him when things are going well. They are always more interested in promises than challenges or correction. Prayer becomes, not so much part of a relationship, but more of a help line to God. Obviously it is good for people to pray under any circumstances, but if we want to grow into spiritual maturity, we need a more permanent relationship with God than that made possible by this 'call-out' procedure.

Nevertheless, St Bernard recognizes that love of God for what he gives has its value. To meet with God under any circumstances gives us an opportunity to discover what he is truly like and causes us to soften with love. 'But and if troubles come one after another, and he betake himself to God and find deliverance every time, though his heart be of stone within a breast of iron, he surely must melt down in gratitude at last'.[4]

God, the Giver, gives something of himself with each gift. The fragrance of his love soaks each new day, the shadow of his presence dances on the walls of our homes, and the touch of his heart is in the hand of all our friendships. In countless ways he seeks to make himself known in the ordinary events that crowd our days. This seems to be his preferred way of doing things. Some seek him through the earthquake, wind and fire; he is to be found more often speaking in a still small voice, awakening our love by the sheer goodness of his presence. To meet with him in each new gift provides the opportunity for our love to grow, so that we begin to seek him, not for his gifts, but for himself. To reject his gifts, or fail to acknowledge that he is the giver, is ultimately to harden our hearts against him. Most of us have experienced the pain of having our love rejected, or our gifts spurned, and know how that damages relationships. We can to some extent enter into God's pain when, as Gift and Giver, he is denied.

Our four children are all either at college or university. Periodically they come home for a weekend, or will arrive at the end of term bearing huge bundles of dirty washing. The washing machine seems to be going for days clearing the back-log of jeans, shirts and socks. One thing my wife refuses to do for any of us, however, is to pair up all the socks after a marathon wash. These are left in a basket for us all to dig around until we find matching pairs. The technique is simple, you locate one of your socks and search for the one that matches. The process can take some time but is obviously important. For every human need God has grace and gifts of his love to match. We can bring the stained, worn, unusable dirtiness of life to him so that he can cleanse us with his healing love and match each of our needs with his grace.

The New Testament occasionally uses a fascinating word, *poikilos*, which means *many-coloured*. It occurs in Peter's first letter when he speaks of the many-coloured grace of God. This is a vivid way of saying that there is no colour in the human situation that the grace of God cannot match. There can be no need, no set of circumstances, no crisis, that the resourceful grace of God cannot deal with. Each new day, if only we could see it, provides us with overwhelming evidence of his inexhaustible desire to give.

Loving God for what he gives is the starting-point for most of us in learning to love him for who he is. But it is surprising how often his gifts are seen as unwelcome, treated with suspicion, or missed altogether. Rejection of his gifts, or failure to recognize the presence of the Giver, and his desire to be known through the gift, can equally prevent us from growing into a mature relationship with him. The second part in the Song of Ascents is the song of praise for the gifts that God showers upon us, thus preparing us for the third stage.

The Love of God for God's Sake

The third degree of love, according to Bernard, is the stage in which God is loved purely for himself. The Christian has learned how wonderful and gracious God is and has a longing to seek him.

> I will get up now and go about the city,
> through its streets and squares;
> I will search for the one my heart loves.
>
> (Song of Songs 3:2)

There is an intimacy with God that transcends human need. The needs of the flesh become a kind of language by which we proclaim joyfully the goodness of God. We love God because we have tasted for ourselves and know how gracious he is. The person who loves like this loves truly, he loves the things of God without self-interest. Bernard, and other mystics, make unashamed use of the language of the lover, they also frequently use similar metaphors; ladder, steps, stages and journey, implying that the Christian life is a pilgrimage. Progress is made by crossing successive thresholds on the way. In *The Dark Night of the Soul*, St John of the Cross explains the steps of the mystic ladder of divine love. 'The fifth step of this ladder of love makes the soul to desire and long for God impatiently. On this step the vehemence of the lover to comprehend the Beloved and be united with Him is such that every delay, however brief, becomes very long, wearisome and oppressive to it . . .'[5]

To be in love, and this is what Bernard, St John of the Cross, and other mystics are on about, is undoubtedly to experience strong and sometimes perplexing emotions. But it is also about joy. Joy is the serious business of heaven, said C. S. Lewis, and the consequence of getting closer to God is a heart lifted by the immense joyfulness of his presence. There is a time to laugh and a time to cry, but dourness has never been a gift of the Spirit. 'Our mouths were filled with laughter, our tongues with songs of joy', so writes the Psalmist in Psalm 126, one of the Songs of Ascents. To love God for himself, to be in love with God, is to know great joy. Not the circumstantial pleasure when everything is going right for us, but a deep, profound experience of our whole being soaked with the joy of God. This is the joy experienced between lover and beloved, it is one of the fruits of the Holy Spirit, and characterizes the Christian pilgrimage. It is said that in order to be canonized in the Roman Catholic Church, there must be proof of joy in the candidate. I feel deeply sorry for those Christians who have interpreted the teachings of Jesus in solemn and humourless tones. They seem unable to experience the joy of their salvation, and appear to expect little more, to use Wordsworth's words, than the 'smile on Duty's face'. One Christian, in her autobiography, speaks of her father who was a Presbyterian elder, as 'being full of rectitude and rigid with duty'. Her impression of him was of a man who 'never committed a pleasure'. What a great shame that people can go through life serving Christ, but finding no real joy in it. This is not his intention at all.

Another impression that is sometimes given is that in order to make progress in the Christian life, to move from one degree of maturity to the next, some form of dehumanization is necessary. I have heard Christians speak with a kind of spiritual language which implies that they are no longer bothered by the sins and weaknesses of the flesh. Growing closer to God does not cancel out our humanity. We remain people, not angels or spirits, and the progress encouraged by St Bernard takes full recognition of the fact that we will continue to experience a battle in some areas of our lives. Holiness is not perfection, but expects and anticipates, the internal conflicts which are so much a part of our search for God. Learning to love God for himself is a process encouraged by our awareness of his unshakeable love for us, despite our sinfulness. He loves us, not despite our humanness, but precisely because of it. Remaining subject to the weaknesses and failures of the flesh does not disqualify us from this process of transformation, nor, miraculously, does it prevent us from drawing ever closer to God.

Even the conflict itself can be a sign that our hearts truly long for God, and gives rise to a desire to be set free to love and serve him. This is how John Donne expressed it:

> Batter my heart, three-person'd God, for you
> As yet but knock, breathe, shine, and seek to mend;
> That I may rise, and stand, o'erthrow me, and bend
> Your force, to break, blow, burn, and make me new.
> I, like an usurp'd town, to another due,
> Labour to' admit you, but O, to no end,
> Reason, your viceroy in me, me should defend,
> But is captiv'd and proves weak or untrue.
> Yet dearly I love you, and would be loved fain,
> But I am betroth'd unto your enemy:
> Divorce me, untie, or break that knot again,
> Take me to you, imprison me, for I,
> Except you enthrall me, never shall be free,
> Nor ever chaste, except you ravish me.[6]

The Love of Self for God's Sake

Among the worst experiences for me at school were the regular cross-country runs. They were compulsory for all unless there was a very good reason why an individual should not run. My memory is of cynical games teachers who treated us all as malingerers. They saw through our pathetic attempts to opt out, and would scathingly reject our carefully forged notes, claiming to be from parents, giving reasons why we should be excused. Hobbling to school as though wounded, headaches and tummyaches were all symptoms treated with contempt. In winter, when the ground was too hard for us to play rugby, we would be sent off mercilessly to complete this miserable exercise. This was a sport at which I did not excel, except for one occasion. We had started a cross-country race, everyone jockeying for position as we ran the first hundred yards across an open field heading for a narrow passage between two hedges at the far corner. For reasons that I have never been able to understand, everyone in front of me headed for the wrong gap, leaving me in the lead as I reached the entrance to the passageway. Because the path was so narrow, and the hedges on either side so dense, other runners, who by now had corrected their mistake and were pounding after me, could not overtake. For a few glorious moments I led the race. I can still remember how wonderful it felt.

Fortunately, the Christian life is not a question of being first past the post. There is plenty of room for the slow, the late starter and the handicapped. Sometimes those who start promisingly get left behind by those whose progress is slower to begin with. Others take the wrong direction earlier on and it takes time to find the right track. We make progress at varying rates, crossing each threshold as we come to it. But there is no competition; those who have travelled further will encourage those still struggling at an earlier stage. The fourth degree, or the fourth verse in our Song of Ascents, where we learn to love ourselves as God loves every person, is, according to Bernard, difficult to achieve. 'Blessed is the man who can attain the fourth degree of love. Then he will love himself only in God . . . For this love is a mountain of great elevation that is fertile and rich.'[7]

To love oneself as God loves every person is a condition so

rare that it is barely attainable in this life. It is to be received
into God and transformed into his likeness. As a drop of water
disappears in a barrel of wine taking the taste and colour of
the wine; as a bar of iron heated red-hot becomes like the
flame; and as air becomes so radiant with the light of the sun
that it appears to be the very sunlight itself; so it is for those
who are absorbed into God. Their human love will be melted
out of them and poured into the love of God. Most of us will
get glimpses of this from time to time, but it is unlikely to be
our permanent state in this life.

To love self as God loves, and to love our neighbour as self
is a call, and a challenge laid before us all. It is a goal to aim
for, but our progress will be interrupted by many defeats. There
will be false starts, wrong turnings, and much heavy going; but
we are in no way to be discouraged. There is no insistence
from Bernard that we all have to reach this final stage in order
to prove we are true Christians. Instead, we are invited to
pursue the goal, recognizing that there will be many glimpses
of heaven on the way, but also many stumbles and even serious
falls. The important thing is to keep going and not to give up.
C. S. Lewis puts it beautifully:

> No amount of falls will really undo us if we keep on picking
> ourselves up each time. We shall of course be very muddy
> and tattered children by the time we reach home. But the
> bathrooms are all ready, the towels put out, and the clean
> clothes in the airing cupboard. The only fatal thing is to lose
> one's temper and give it up. It is when we notice the dirt
> that God is most present in us: it is the very sign of his
> presence.[8]

This perfection of love can only be completely experienced at
the resurrection. It is the final threshold across which we step
into the pure light of God's immediate presence. It is at this
moment that we shall meet face to face the One who has
walked with us through the years, picking us up when we have

fallen, whispering encouragement to us when we would have given up. Simultaneously, we will understand both the object and the process of our pilgrimage, and will rejoice with all those who have sung their song of ascents as they have crossed one threshold after another and live now fully and utterly in Christ. This final threshold is the point at which we will understand the reality of the words St Paul speaks when he declares his certainty in the fact that nothing will be able to separate us from the love of Christ. We will see blindingly clearly that this has always been true, even during our most painful times of desolation when we felt out of the running altogether. We will be able to piece together the clues laid patiently and consistently in our path, and see the great master plan. The secret will be revealed, and we will enter into total oneness with our God and with ourselves. If it is possible to feel loss at this moment, we will feel the loss of wasted years when we could have taken so many things for granted. His love, our self-worth, the certainty and precision of his guiding hand concealed in all of the perplexing events of our disturbed lives. Christ, the door, the final and ultimate threshold, waits at the end of all our years to receive us home. We will not be chided, but we will have this great sense that it could all have been so different. If only we could have trusted, instead of doubted, his power to hold us. If only we could have rested in his overwhelming love, our passageway would have been so much easier with each threshold negotiated in security and peace.

This is the reality that can change the way people live. So many say, 'if only I knew what lay ahead'. But we do know. We know the unshakeable love of Christ, we know that nothing can cut us off from his presence, nothing prevent us from making it to our destination. Francis of Sales has said, 'After the journey to God, there is a journey in God'. The moment of commitment, the moment of understanding, brings us to the first threshold. Thereafter, our journey is in God keeping company with the most unlikely characters. The Threshold People move hesitantly together towards the final glorious threshold of resurrection. This journey in God is one of breath-taking discovery as we allow Jesus to lead us through the frightening marginal areas of our lives to redeem, by his wounded love, the scarred, blackened memories and experiences that have cast such a shadow across our path. The final triumphant song links earth with heaven, it is a glorious, exhilarating acclamation as the summit is reached. There have been many satisfying sightings on the way, many words of encouragement from fellow travellers, many divine nudges in the right direction, but at last our song can be joined into the full-throated roar of heaven.

There the fourth degree of love is attained forever. It consists of loving God, only and always. Then we shall not even love ourselves, except as we do for God's own sake. For God will be the reward of them that love Him. Then God will be the everlasting reward of an eternal love.[9]

Notes

Chapter 2: A Ridiculous Love

1. John V. Taylor, *The Go-Between God* (SCM, London 1972), p. 172.
2. Quoted in the *Norton Anthology of English Literature* (Norton, New York 1962), vol. 2, pp. 1053–7, and in many anthologies.
3. Simone Weil, *Gateway to God* (Collins/Fount Paperback, Glasgow 1974), p. 87.
4. *Dark Night of the Soul*, trans. by E. Allison Peers (Burns and Oates, Tunbridge Wells 1976), pp. 27–8.

Chapter 3: Downwardly Mobile

1. Martin Luther, 'Treatise on Christian Liberty', in *Works*, II 342 (Muhlenberg Press, Philadelphia 1943).
2. Alexander Solzhenitsyn, *The Gulag Archipelago*, III–IV (Harper and Row, New York 1975) pp. 615–16.
3. Otto Baab, *The Theology of the Old Testament* (Abingdon-Cokesbury, New York 1949), pp. 105, 110.

Chapter 4: Strength and Weakness

1. Dr Paul Tournier, *The Strong and the Weak* (SCM, London 1963), p. 21.
2. Stephen Verney, *The Dance of Love* (Fount, London 1989), p. 80.
3. C. S. Lewis, *Prince Caspian* (Puffin, Harmondsworth 1962), p. 185.

4. Père de la Columbière, quoted by Brennan Manning TOR, *The Gentle Revolutionaries* (Dimension Books, New Jersey 1976), p. 129.
5. Robert Girard, *My Weakness His Strength* (Zondervan, 1981), p. 148.
6. Henri Nouwen, *Creative Ministry* (Doubleday, New York 1991), p. 113.
7. Henri Nouwen, *Reaching Out* (Collins, 1976), p. 36.

Chapter 5: The Void of Loneliness

1. Rubin Gotesky, 'Aloneness, Loneliness, Isolation, Solitude', in *An Invitation to Phenomenology*, edited by James Edie (Quadrangle Books, Chicago 1965), pp. 211–40.
2. Dr Paul Tournier, *Escape From Loneliness* (Highland Books, Crowborough 1983), p. 31.
3. *The Confessions of St Augustine*, in the translation of Sir Tobie Matthew KT, revised by Dom Roger Hudleston (Collins/Fontana Books, London 1957), p. 31.
4. Dietrich Bonhoeffer, *Life Together* (Harper and Row, New York 1952), pp. 77, 78.
5. Kahlil Gibran, *The Prophet* (Heinemann, London 1926), pp. 16–19.
6. Dag Hammarskjöld, *Markings*, trans. by Leif Sjöberg and W. H. Auden (Faber and Faber, London 1964), p. 134.
7. Catherine de Hueck Doherty, *Poustinia, Christian Spirituality of the East for Western Man* (Fount Paperbacks, London 1977).
8. Thomas à Kempis, *The Imitation of Christ* (Penguin, Harmondsworth 1952), p. 50.
9. Adrian Plass, *The Sacred Diary of Adrian Plass* (Marshall Pickering, Basingstoke 1987), pp. 89, 90.

Chapter 6: The Journey in God

1. Gerard Manley Hopkins, 'The habit of perfection', in *A Selection of Poems and Prose* (Penguin 1953).
2. *Writings from the Philokalia on Prayer of the Heart*, trans. by E.

Kadloubovsky and G. E. H. Palmer (Faber and Faber, London 1954), p. 33.

3. St John of the Cross, *The Living Flame of Love*, Commentary on Stanza 3, No 18. (For a translation see: Kieran Kavanaugh and Otilio Rodriguez, *The Collected Works of St John of the Cross*, Washington D.C., ICS Publications, Institute of Carmelite Studies 1973), pp. 617ff.

4. Jacques Ellul, *False Presence of the Kingdom*, trans. by C. Edward Hopkin (The Seabury Press, New York 1972), p. 85.

5. Henri J. M. Nouwen, *Reaching Out* (Collins/Fount Paperbacks, Glasgow 1980), p. 35.

6. Carlo Carretto, *The Desert in the City* (Collins/Fount Paperbacks 1981), p. 19.

7. Brother Lawrence, *The Practice of the Presence of God* (Spire Books 1958), p. 29.

8. Kahlil Gibran, *The Prophet* (Heinemann, London 1926), p. 69.

9. *The Sign of Jonas* (Burns and Oates, London 1953), p. 261. Quoted by Henri J. M. Nouwen in *Reaching Out* (Collins/Fount Paperbacks, Glasgow 1980), p. 42.

Chapter 7: Defeating Giants

1. Stephen Pile, *The Book of Heroic Failures* (Routledge and Kegan Paul Ltd, London 1979).

2. Isaac M. Marks MD, *Living with Fear* (McGraw-Hill, New York 1978), p. 9.

3. Dietrich Bonhoeffer, quoted by Eugene Peterson in *A Long Obedience in the Same Direction* (Marshall-Pickering, London 1989), p. 32.

Chapter 8: Sexuality and Spirituality

1. Karen Armstrong, *The Gospel According to Woman* (Pan Books, London 1987).

2. Louis Lavelle, *The Meaning of Holiness* (Burns and Oates, London 1951), pp. 1, 2.

3. Peter Brown, *The Body and Society* (Faber and Faber, London 1989), p. 33.
4. Ibid., p. 34.

Chapter 9: The Song of Ascents

1. Bernard of Clairvaux, *The Love of God*, edited by James M. Houston (Pickering and Inglis, Basingstoke 1983), editor's note xix.
2. Paul Vitz, *Psychology as Religion – The Cult of Self Worship* (Lion Publishing, Tring 1979).
3. Ludwig Feuerbach, quoted by Paul Vitz, ibid., p. 66.
4. St Bernard, *On the Love of God*, *De Diligendo Deo*, trans. by a Religious of CSMV (A. R. Mowbray, London 1950), p. 42.
5. St John of the Cross, *The Dark Night of the Soul*, trans. by E. Allison Peers (Burns and Oates, Tunbridge Wells 1976), p. 165.
6. John Donne, 'Holy Sonnet XIV', *Complete Poetry and Selected Prose*, edited by John Hayward (The Nonesuch Press, London 1967), p. 285.
7. Bernard of Clairvaux, op. cit., p. 158.
8. C. S. Lewis, *The Business of Heaven* (Collins, London 1984), p. 17.
9. Bernard of Clairvaux, op. cit., p. 163.

Further Reading

Blaise Arminjon sj, *The Cantata of Love*, translated by Nelly Marans (Ignatius Press, San Francisco 1988). This book, by a Jesuit who is a renowned master of the Spiritual Exercises of St Ignatius, is a verse by verse reading of the Song of Songs.

Bernard of Clairvaux, *The Love of God*, abridged, edited, and introduced by James M. Houston (Pickering and Inglis, Basingstoke 1983). A good introduction to the life and writing of St Bernard.

Peter Brown, *The Body and Society* (Faber and Faber, London 1990). This book is an exploration of the theme of sexual renunciation by both men and women in early Christianity.

Carlo Carretto, *In Search of the Beyond*, translated by Sarah Fawcett (Darton, Longman and Todd, London 1975). Carlo Carretto found the solitude of the Sahara desert an inspiration to prayer. He encourages each person to create a 'desert' into which we can withdraw to pray.

Catherine de Hueck Doherty, *Poustinia* (Collins, Glasgow 1977). Subtitled *Christian Spirituality of the East for Western Man*, the book brings the insights, traditions and spirituality of the Russian Orthodox Church to the West. The Russian word *poustinia*, meaning desert, is a quiet, lonely place to which we can withdraw to find the God who dwells within us.

Kahlil Gibran, *The Prophet* (Heinemann, London 1926). A poetic, artistic, beautiful book coming out of Eastern spirituality, which speaks with moving clarity to our spiritual needs.

Gerard W. Hughes, *God of Surprises* (Darton, Longman and Todd, London 1985). Quoting from the author's preface, 'This book has only one purpose – to suggest some ways of detecting the hidden treasure in what you may consider a most unlikely field, yourself'.

Morton T. Kelsey, *The Other Side of Silence*, (SPCK, London 1977). A practical book for those who would like to learn how to do Christian meditation.

Thomas à Kempis, *The Imitation of Christ*, translated and introduced by Leo Sherley-Price (Penguin, Middlesex 1952). A spiritual classic in which the themes of the love, mercy and holiness of God are worked out in practical counsels to guide and inspire.

Brother Lawrence, *The Practice of the Presence of God* (The Upper Room Publishing Co., Nashville 1950). The title of the book speaks for itself.

Margaret Magdalene, *Transformed by Love* (Darton, Longman and Todd, London 1989). A compelling exposition of the life of Mary Magdalene which calls us to love more passionately.

Henri J. M. Nouwen, *Reaching Out* (Collins, Glasgow 1976). Sub-titled *The Three Movements of the Spiritual Life*, this book offers spiritual insight expressed in terms of movement; from loneliness to solitude, hostility to hospitality, and illusion to prayer.

Ronald Rolheiser, *The Restless Heart* (Hodder and Stoughton, London 1988). A helpful book for those trying to understand loneliness, it contains guidelines to enable us to use it creatively.

Anthony Storr, *Solitude* (Flamingo, London 1989). A positive and creative approach to solitude. The capacity to be alone is seen as a sign of maturity.

Stephen Verney, *The Dance of Love* (Collins, London 1989). The author, former Bishop of Repton, looks at the original meaning of some Christian words and shows how they can be used to relate the two sides of our nature, the human and the divine.

St John of the Cross, *The Dark Night of the Soul*, translated by E. Allison Peers (Burns and Oates, Tunbridge Wells 1976). One of the best known spiritual classics of all time.

Paul Tournier, *The Strong and the Weak* (SCM Press, London 1963). Dr Tournier maintains that people should not be classified as strong or weak, we are all strong towards some and weak towards others. He writes to enable us all to learn psychological courage and spiritual wisdom.

Paul Tournier, *Escape From Loneliness* (Highland Books, Crowborough 1983). The author addresses the problem of emotional isolation and offers the hope of healing through true fellowship.

Paul C. Vitz, *Psychology as Religion – The Cult of Self Worship* (Lion, Tring 1979). A forthright critique of modern psychology, this book challenges the cult of selfism and presents a realistic Christian understanding of the problems of human nature.

Simone Weil, *Gateway to God* (Collins, Glasgow 1974). In his foreword Malcolm Muggeridge describes Simone Weil as a pilgrim of the absolute who gives God's love a homely and familiar face. It is a book that will help other pilgrims as they struggle to negotiate their personal thresholds.